"HOLD UP YOUR LIGHT"

"HOLD UP YOUR LIGHT"

Vaughn J. Featherstone

Bookcraft

Salt Lake City, Utah

Library of Congress Catalog Card Number: 86-71251
ISBN 0-88494-600-2

2nd Printing, 1987

Printed in the United States of America

To
my daughter Jill,
my son Paul,
and
my grandchildren
as a guide to them along life's journey,
as an expression of the values I hold dear,
and as an encouragement to develop total
unity, purity, and charity

Contents

Preface

Some years back Bookcraft invited me to write a book for leaders of Latter-day Saint youth. Delighted with this privilege, I prepared a manuscript which was later published under the title *A Generation of Excellence*.

Almost before the ink was dry on the pages, the publisher reported the response from stores: They understood the need for a book to the leaders of youth, but there was also a great need for a book to the young people. Would I write such a book? My book *Do-It-Yourself Destiny* was published two years later.

Several years have elapsed since then. Now I feel a need among youth and their leaders for a strong guide during these difficult times we live in. The present book is an expression of teachings that can help this generation and their exemplars prepare themselves against the adversary in this time and season. This book includes the values that I want to become part of the lives of my own children and grandchildren.

I am appreciative to many people for their help with this book, but most especially to Carol Steffensen, who typed the manuscript and assisted in many other ways. I express appreciation to Bookcraft for their willingness to publish it.

I am especially grateful to George Bickerstaff, Bookcraft's editor-in-chief, for his exacting care in editing the manuscript and overseeing the book's production.

This is not an official publication of The Church of Jesus Christ of Latter-day Saints. It represents the personal feelings, opinions, and principles which I think might give some direction to the lives of our young people and those who lead the youth (including priesthood leaders, parents, advisers, and teachers), but especially to the youth themselves. It is my hope that they will find in it much that will assist them during a period in their life when perhaps they need special guidance and direction.

PART ONE

BECOME
A STANDARD

Answering a Call to Arms

Moroni, who was the chief commander of the armies of the Nephites,

> rent his coat; and he took a piece thereof, and wrote upon it—In memory of our God, our religion, and freedom, and our peace, our wives, and our children—and he fastened it upon the end of a pole.
>
> And he fastened on his headplate, and his breastplate, and his shields, and girded on his armor about his loins; and he took the pole, which had on the end thereof his rent coat, (and he called it the title of liberty) and he bowed himself to the earth, and he prayed mightily unto his God for the blessings of liberty to rest upon his brethren, so long as there should a band of Christians remain to possess the land—
>
> And . . . Moroni . . . went forth among the people, waving the rent part of his garment in the air, that all might see the writing which he had written upon the rent part, and crying with a loud voice, saying:
>
> Behold, whosoever will maintain this title upon the land, let them come forth in the strength of the Lord, and enter into a covenant that they will maintain their rights, and their religion, that the Lord God may bless them. (Alma 46:12–13, 19–20.)

This is the day and we are issuing the call to you our beloved youth of the Church of Jesus Christ. You are the band of Christians. This is a rallying call. Come forth, the battle is at hand. Never has enlistment in the Lord's cause been so great.

The standard for you has been erected. The trump has sounded clear and terrible. The battle lines have been drawn. The evening is at hand. Lucifer's army is marshalled in ranks of evil and satanic forces. Darkness is descending over the land. Evil abounds on every side. Their battle cry is fearful and they give no quarter. Their cause is destruction, sin, death, and hell. They have only one cause, and all the powers of evil on earth and in hell are combining against "the band of Christians." They serve the devil and list to do his will. Their soldiers are myriad and they form in terrible ranks of darkness and evil.

But the Lord has sent forth the greatest and mightiest leaders of all time and he counsels us, "But first let my army become very great, and let it be sanctified before me, that it may become fair as the sun, and clear as the moon, and that her banners may be terrible unto all nations" (D&C 105:31). This is a time of choice— "choose ye this day whom ye will serve." Christ is at our head. Our commander-in-chief is the President of this Church. The Lord has called his generals and captains from among the good and holy men and women of the kingdom; people of sound understanding and of truth and soberness; of integrity and loyalty; people who will fight for the cause of the Master. These people are filled with justice and mercy. They are filled with light, and they trust in the Lord their God and know he will deliver us.

We call you to join the ranks. As young David challenged, "Is there not a cause?" Oh, my beloved youth, there is a cause and it is glorious beyond description. We are waging war for the souls of the children of men. Our message is peace, charity, purity, and obedience. Our generation is expected to go forth as the "children of Light" in meekness and humility with the power of God. We must penetrate every nation, visit every clime, sweep every country, and sound in every ear, remembering that no unhallowed hand can stop the work from progressing.

It is time for Zion to put on its beautiful garments as a contrast to the evil army which is clothed in dark, evil, and loathsome attire. We will become fair as the sun and clear as the moon. Purge and purify your lives. Live every commandment. Cease to be idle. Learn to work. Live the Word of Wisdom. Do not ensnare yourselves in the lusts of the flesh. Discipline your lives. Avoid compromises in music, dance, and dress. Seek to become pure in heart and to be obedient in all things. Remove every particle of rebellion (which comes from Satan) from your souls. Honor your fathers and mothers.

Learn of the Lord and his strategy for his army. Study the scriptures daily. Read the Book of Mormon with a prayerful heart. Pray in secret and with your families. Learn to have absolute and complete trust in the Lord.

When we do this, Satan cannot prevail. Youth, young adults, leaders, and parents—this is a call to arms. Let us swell the ranks of God. Let us go out after those who have not enlisted who may be deceived, who are in "no man's land" spiritually—those who may have wounded spirits and who are being enticed by the evil one. Let us here resolve that every particle of energy and every possible method shall be devised to swell our ranks with hosts of unknown soldiers who are inactive and who need a cause greater than the present compromising position in which they find themselves.

Let us go in search of them. Let us start with the Primary and challenge every Primary president to activate two boys and two girls this year. Let us challenge every deacon, teacher, and priest quorum to activate at least one quorum member this year. Let us ordain two additional priests to the office of elder and let the sisters likewise reach out to the ranks of the young women.

Brethren, this strategy will swell the ranks of the Aaronic Priesthood with over one quarter of a million modern soldiers of God, and within three years we will have fifty thousand missionaries. "Is there not a cause?"

A Roman general, Lucius Aemilius Paulus, surnamed Macedonicus, said:

> Commanders should be counselled chiefly by persons of known talent, by those who have made the art of war their particular study, and whose knowledge is derived from experience, by those who are present at the scene of the action, who see the enemy, who see the advantages that occasions offer, and who, like people embarked in the same ship are sharers of the danger.
>
> If, therefore, anyone thinks himself qualified to give advice respecting the war which I am about to conduct, let him not refuse his assistance to the state, but let him come with me into Macedonia.

He shall be furnished with a ship, a tent, even his travelling charges will be defrayed, but if he thinks this too much trouble, and prefers the repose of a city life to the toils of war, let him not on land assume the office of a pilot. The city in itself furnishes abundance of topics for conversation; let it confine its passion for talking to its own precincts and rest assured that we shall pay no attention to any counsel but such as shall be framed within our camp.

I have seen the enemy. He is real and I have been at the scene of action. We need youth who can stand the heat. The refiner's fire is celestial heat. It will require self-mastery, discipline, and control of our appetites. It will require sacrifice. When an athlete makes a decision to play high school ball or compete in any way in athletics, he commits to certain rules and disciplines. When you join the Lord's army, there are disciplines and sacrifices. Always remember that the rewards and blessings come to those who participate.

Come, my beloved young friends, let us rise and shine forth as fair as the sun and clear as the moon. Let the Lord's army become very great, then let us move forward with a power never known in the history of the world. We will carry the title of liberty and the gospel of Jesus Christ with great honor. The band of Christians will swell and become the mighty army of God, and this day the Lord will deliver the enemy into our hands. We will win and the victory will be sweet. We will hold to the iron rod and we will partake of the fruit of the tree of life.

Listen. Can you hear it off in the distance? The trumpet is sounding. Can you hear the clarion call? Can you hear the pounding steps of the marching armies of God? They are coming; rise up, give a battle shout, and join their ranks.

"The Standard of Truth has been erected; no unhallowed hand can stop the work from progressing; persecutions may rage, mobs may combine, armies may assemble, calumny may defame, but the truth of God will go forth boldly, nobly and independent, till it has penetrated every continent, visited every clime, swept every country, and sounded in every ear, till the purposes of God shall be accomplished, and the Great Jehovah shall say the work is done" (Joseph Smith, *History of the Church*, 4:540).

Serving with Compassion

Compassion is charity. Those who are filled with it are ever alert to follow in the footsteps of the Master. Compassion requires a degree of selflessness that few possess. It causes us to put the needs of others before many things that we would do which are of a lesser nature.

A district Scout executive years ago organized a Cub pack at a training school. Many of those who had been institutionalized at this school were mentally limited. With the approval of the Boy Scouts of America, men and boys whose mental development would not exceed twelve years of age, and was generally much less, were registered in the Cub Scouts. The pack grew to approximately fifty members. This would be about five dens. The district executive worked with the boys, found volunteer leaders, had uniforms donated, and gave every soul a Cub Scout experience. One of these men was eighty-three years old. He had the mind of a child and had been at the training school for eighty years.

The executive challenged the Cubs to advance to be perfect in uniform inspection, and he generally made the experience fun and exciting for the group. One year during charter review the pack was to have a uniform inspection.

The executive lined each den up. Every Cub thought he would merit a full 100 percent toward the inspection. Everyone was in full uniform. The Scout executive said in jest: "I'll bet I can find something wrong. You couldn't all be 100 percent." He methodically inspected every Cub in each den. He graded them perfect until he came to the last den. The eighty-three-year-old Cub was in that den in his wheelchair. This old man was radiant, feeling he also would receive a 100 percent appraisal. The executive inspected him carefully, then he smiled and said, "I think I found something that keeps the pack from having 100 percent." The old man's face dropped. Tears welled up in his eyes. The executive said, "You haven't shaved." The eighty-three-year-old man said: "They will not give me a razor. No one cares to shave me." And then the tears worked their way down his cheeks.

The executive opened up his book and acted as if he were checking, then he said: "I made a mistake. I can't find anyplace where it says a Cub Scout has to shave. I give you all 100 percent."

A light came to the old man's eyes, a great smile burst forth, and the tears vanished. Soon the eighty-three-year-old Cub Scout graduated from the training school into a rest home. The only thing he took with him was his Cub Scout uniform. What a great story of pride and compassion!

Fred Day, who is the Chief Scout Executive in the Provo area, told of his young son receiving his first Cub Scout uniform. He put it on to go to his first pack meeting. The dad went out and got in the car and suggested that the boy come with him. His son said, "I am going to walk to the meeting tonight." The father drove over to the chapel and his eight-year-old son walked right down the middle of the street to the chapel. He wanted everyone to see his Cub Scout uniform. He wore the uniform for the duration of the time he was in the Cub Scouts. He drowned in an unusual accident a year later.

For his burial they dressed him in his Cub Scout uniform, which by this time had a hole in one knee. His father said that someone had suggested that the boy be outfitted in a new uniform, but the family refused because this was the one their son loved so well.

These thoughtful parents had the compassion to bury their son in the little uniform in which he felt such great pride.

I remember also hearing about a woman who raised her family alone. She worked to pay for their missions and college education. She had gone to school herself and studied world geography. She had read about all the marvelous places in the world. Finally, after all her children were raised, she decided to go on a world cruise. She worked for months and finally saved enough money to pay her fare.

She barely had enough money to pay for her ticket, so she decided to fill one suitcase with cheese and crackers and eat in her cabin. Each time the meal hour approached she went to her room and ate cheese and crackers. On the final night of the cruise the captain had a special dinner for all the guests. He invited this little widow to sit at his table. She was embarrassed and declined the invitation and went to her cabin. Soon the captain knocked on her door and wanted to know if she was not feeling well. In entering her room he saw the portion of cheese and crackers she had prepared for her meal. She was embarrassed but said: "I had only enough money to pay for my ticket. There was not sufficient to pay for my meals, so I filled a suitcase with cheese and crackers. It was worth it. It has been one of the most thrilling experiences of my life." She talked about all that she had seen, her eyes aglow.

When she finished, he said to her: "Did you not know that all of the meals came with the purchase of the ticket. You could have eaten without any cost to you. Didn't anyone explain that to you?" She was shocked to learn this, but said: "I have no regrets. It has been wonderful, more beautiful than I ever would have supposed. It has been the fulfillment of a lifetime dream."

This wonderful woman had a perspective about things that should teach us all a real lesson. She did not let her misunderstanding detract from all the positive, beautiful things that had transpired.

Youth can develop compassion in a multitude of ways. It takes maturity to be a compassionate person. The best place to practice compassion is among the members of the family.

When I was growing up, I lived in a home where we were very

dependent on each other. We somehow, without recognizing it, practiced this sacred trait of compassion. I suppose it was because we were concerned for each other and realized the embarrassment we each faced. There was little money to spend on food or clothing. Our clothes were often passed on to us from neighbors or from older brothers and sisters.

My older brother has always been a hero in my life. He used to work at Seagull Bakery. It was several miles from home. He rode his bike to work in the evening and worked until about two-thirty in the morning. He was up for school at the regular time. I never heard him complain, and by working in that way he was able to buy some better clothes.

He had one shirt, a long-sleeved, semi-dress shirt, that was dark blue. I borrowed it permanently. I washed it every night and ironed it every morning. The only change of shirts I had was to occasionally wear a white T-shirt. My brother and I seemed to have a special feeling for each other and a common concern.

How can seven children not feel compassion for a mother who puts on heavy men's shoes, men's clothes, and then works at a smelter like a man, from 10:00 P.M. to 6:00 A.M.? Our mother arrived home about seven in the morning to get us up for school. Then she did the washing, ironing, and baking, cleaned the house, and fixed the meals for us. I do not know when the poor woman slept.

I cannot describe in words the tender and compassionate feelings I have for her to this day. She was always there. In spite of the trials we faced, we had a sense of security because we anchored our lives to a woman who loved us and who we knew would never leave us.

You can practice compassion in serving and helping your older brothers and sisters and in assisting those younger than you. I never remember my older brother telling me I could not wear his shirt. He somehow understood my needs and never complained. I was elected junior and senior class president in high school and always felt that somehow it was because of him. He was popular in high school, played football, and was on the track team, and his reputation carried over, I think perhaps I reaped the benefits.

Your family needs may vary from ours, but individuals always will respond to compassionate service. Compassionate service is generated from the heart. Select a different family member every day and perform some act of compassionate service. You will soon develop a habit of being aware of those who need a helping hand.

Robert Ingersoll, an atheist, said, "The hands that help are holier than the lips that pray." I agree with that, if all one does is pray. However, when the lips that pray and the hands that help are the same person's, then our service is God inspired. God bless us to be compassionate to our fellow beings and to have a righteous pride in who we are and what we can accomplish.

Performing and Achieving

N$_{\text{o}}$ matter how valid, excuse never changes performance." These words I read years back in a book by Lynn Fluckiger entitled *Dynamic Leadership*. I have since come to appreciate those who are able to achieve regardless of circumstance. Petronius Arbiter stated this in A.D. 66:

> We trained hard—but it seemed that every time we were beginning to form up into teams, we would be reorganized. I was to learn that later in life we tend to meet any new situation by reorganizing, and a wonderful method it can be for creating the illusion of progress while producing confusion, inefficiency and demoralization.

Those who succeed do so because they apply certain principles. Earl Nightingale, on the regular program of Mountain Fuel Supply's evening commentary, observed:

> Charles Garfield is a revolving genius, apparently. Still in his late thirties, he holds doctorates in mathematics and psychology. He lifted weights at trials for the U.S. Olympic team. As a mathematician and computer analyst, he helped design the first lunar module and plot its course to the moon. He is now president of the Peak Performance Center in Berkeley and a clinical professor at the University of California at San Francisco Medical School. He is not, we might venture to say, your typical guy. I'm happy to say I've had

several long talks with Charles Garfield and, in addition to everything else he's managed to do, he's a very nice person. We're at present working on a program he wants to do for our company. His main interest in life is the peak performer—the person, man or woman, who is not content to just go along with the great swarm. Furthermore, Charles Garfield thinks that the ingredients of peak performance can be taught to those who would like to raise their levels of performance but don't know how, or are perhaps a bit concerned about what would happen if they did.

Garfield suggests that there are eight main characteristics of the peak performer. The first is that he or she has a passionate mission of some kind. Peak performers have an intense commitment to something; they approach it with what Garfield calls "intentionality and delight."

The second is a willingness to collaborate. Peak performers tend more toward a cooperative than a secretive or competitive style. They know how, when, and where to ask for support. (I'd like to add here that people with a good self-image aren't concerned about competition.)

The third characteristic of the peak performer is that he or she is not obsessed with perfection. The peak performer is willing to use mistakes as a source of information for self-correction.

Number four, [they] master the core skills in their fields of endeavor. The peak performer quickly discovers what the basics are and masters them. They target most of the work energy here rather than into less important areas.

Five, set your priorities well. When it comes to arranging time, peak performers have a keen sense of what's most important. Six, take risks. Peak performers consistently extend themselves beyond their own personal "comfort zones," out of their habitual roles or environments. Seven, Learn to relax and reflect. Know how to handle or deflect stress; take stock regularly and allow time off. Contrary to what you may think, the peak performer is not the workaholic—far from it.

Let's see, that was seven—relax and reflect. And eight . . . visualize! Imagine yourself performing successfully. "To use this master skill," Garfield says, "you have to learn to relax enough to plant images deep down in your brain. Once you have the images of excellent performance, whether it's in a sport or on a job, you'll begin to perform that way."

Which of the eight characteristics of the peak performer is most difficult of attainment? In today's world, I might venture the guess that it would be number one: Having a passionate interest. ("Have a Passionate Mission," reprinted with permission of the Nightingale-Conant Corporation, Chicago, 1982 copyright, producers of the Earl Nightingale Radio Program, "Our Changing World.")

These eight rules are important to getting results. Believe that you really can make a difference.

Although it may be rough on you, pray for someone who will risk your friendship to help you. These special friends are few and far between. They will need a Christlike love to want to help or correct you more than they want your friendship. These people know that someday, sometime the true spirit in their hearts will be made known to you and you will be grateful.

I remember a ward coach who was umpiring a ward baseball game. I came to bat. The pitcher threw several fastballs. Each time the umpire called a strike. I was certain he was mistaken. By the time I had come to bat several times and he had called at least a dozen strikes on me that I knew were way outside, I started to resent him. I did not say anything, I just held it all in. After the game he came to me and said: "Vaughn, you are standing deep in the batter's box. I know you thought the pitches were all balls but they were right over. Are you afraid of the ball, afraid of getting hit?" I said, "No." He suggested that I stand closer to the plate.

For years I always felt that he had misjudged and had not called the game accurately. Finally, while playing fast-pitch softball, I was not hitting as well as I should and stepped closer to the plate. I began to hit; he had been right all the time. Possibly subconsciously I was afraid of the ball. He was willing to risk offense to help me. I was offended but now I appreciate what he tried to do for me.

E. Grady Bogue, Chancellor of Louisiana State University in Shreveport, told of an incident in his young life:

> In 1952, I played first French horn in the Blue Band at Dixie Music Camp held at Arkansas A&M College in Monticello, Arkansas, now the University of Arkansas at Monticello. The director of the Blue Band, the camp's most advanced band, was an unforgettable personality.
>
> Scrubby Watson was a short, rotund fellow from Pine Bluff, Arkansas. It is probable that the Coca Cola bottling plant in Pine Bluff used Scrubby as a model for their short bottles. He had one or two fingers withered from an overexposure to X-rays in the early history of that diagnostic tool. One glass eye had the disturbing habit of wandering around the rehearsal hall while the one good eye remained fixed on the music and musicians. And on the grand finale concert, ended each year with Sousa's "Stars and Stripes Forever,"

Scrubby would forsake all dignity on the podium, turning to the audience and imitating with baton-to-mouth the technical flourishes of the piccolos.

I had won over the first chair of the Arkansas State Band that year, to be the first chair in the Blue Band. I thought I was pretty good. One day we were making our way through Wagner's "Siegfried's Rhine Journey." Now for those of you who keep cultural company with Ray Fox, Leon Hess and Bill Price, let me note that this is not a refrain from Foggy Mountain Breakdown nor music to clog by.

When we arrived at the solo part, I splattered bad notes all over the rehearsal hall, and they came leaking down the walls, like a busted bottle of musical catsup. Not willing or wanting to let this mortifying performance pass, Scrubby stopped the band in mid phrase, fixed the one good eye on me and said: "Uh huh, uh huh. You've been telling all the girls what a hot shot horn player you are and here you are wandering around the music like a blind dog in a meat factory."

Folks, this was a hot moment of embarrassment in my young life and I yearned for the ability to slither away. That week I took to the shade trees for practice and rendered a near perfect solo on the Friday evening concert. I still remember the warm thrill of mastery and the painful moment of discipline it took to produce it.

Scrubby Watson was a leader in my life. He enjoys a moment of immortality because that act of caring and correction lives on in my life. ("The Flogging of Theagenes: A Poverty of Leadership Vision," *Vital Speeches of the Day* [Southold, New York: City News Publishing Co.], p. 597.)

Emerson, in his essay on compensation, said: "As no man had ever a point of pride that was not injurious to him, so no man had ever a defect that was not somewhere made useful to him. Has he a defect of temper that unfits him to live in society? Thereby he is driven to entertain himself alone and acquire habits of self-help; and thus, like the wounded oyster, he mends his shell with a pearl." (As quoted in Bogue, "The Flogging of Theagenes," p. 597.)

We have all read the statement by Francis Bacon, "It is a sad fate for a man to die too well known to others and still unknown to himself" (as quoted in Bogue, "The Flogging of Theagenes," p. 597).

This Church needs men and women who are self-disciplined, who have enough faith to get the job done. We must help each other become performance oriented. The Lord never intended for us to be failures in what we do.

Every day we brush against great souls. This is especially true in the Church. We can learn from those around us. Listen to the small talk of great men and the great talk of small men.

When we learn how to get results we are assured success in any field of endeavor we choose. The application of true principles brings positive results.

Seventeen hundred years before the American Revolution, Seneca said, "It is to the interest of the commonwealth of mankind that there should be someone who is unconquered, someone against whom fortune has no power."

Years ago I had a security man talk to our corporate executives. During his presentation he said, "Every man, every woman has a price. For some it is money, for others it is power or influence. It may be a woman, possessions, etc." Then he went on to discuss that no one can really be trusted if *his* price is paid. In other words, it was his belief that no one could be totally trusted under all conditions. I thought about the men who preside over the Church, the stakes and wards, and knew that he was mistaken. Every man does not have his price. (Such a belief does, however, tell you a lot about the speaker.)

Great men and women will always make waves. In his speech to the Canadian Senate and House of Commons, December 30, 1941, Winston Churchill said, "We have not journeyed all this way across the centuries, across the oceans, across the mountains, across the prairies, because we are made of sugar candy." And, President Harrison once said: "In America, a glorious fire has been lighted upon the altar of liberty. Keep it burning; and let the sparks that continually go up from it fall on other altars, and light up in distance lands the fire of freedom." (As quoted by Ronald Reagan in his address to the International Longshoremen's Association, July 18, 1983, the Diplomat Convention Hall, Hollywood, Florida: The White House Office of the Press Secretary, p. 8).

This Church has worked miracles in the lives of the people who live the gospel. I saw families in west Texas living in cardboard-walled homes. The children were ragged, unclean, poor, and had no clothes to wear to church. Then I saw a trans-formation take place when they joined the Church. In a short time all the family had Sunday clothes, they moved into a modest home, and they were no longer poor. The Lord blessed them as they performed.

We find changes like this in the lives of people who are committed and converted.

Now one word of warning. Our results must be in the things the Lord would have us succeed in. We must use wisdom and remember that Satan will also attempt to use people who can get results. He is not much interested in drones who never do anything. He also wants to enlist performance-oriented people who can destroy as others build.

Stuart Clark Rogers gave us this interesting insight when he said:

> Tyranny does not always march in the night in hobnail boots. Tyranny today is more likely to jog up to you on a sunny day in a pair of Adidas, and remark pleasantly, "Gosh, old pal, wouldn't it be nice if we could *do* something for all those people who aren't as clever as *we* are. Let's protect them from their own fooishness. Let's see to it that they're only exposed to what they really *need* to know. And let's *punish* those we *think* might be able to take advantage of them." ("Freedom Needs Advertising: Access to Information, Defense of Our Rights," *Vital Speeches of the Day,* vol. 51, no. 3 [Southold, New York: City News Publishing Co., 1984], p. 89; copyright by S. C. Rogers, Inc., Englewood, Colorado.)

There will always be a clue to those who pervert the Lord's true principles of performance and achievement. They will not feel at peace with the Spirit.

Now, we as a church must move forward with a great resolve to move the kingdom forward. The Lord expects it and we will do it. God bless us to perform as he would have us.

CHAPTER FOUR

Stretching the Mind

Claude C. Cox, in Atlanta, Georgia, at the National Conference of Broadcast Ministries, used the phrase "motivating the clogged brain" (*Vital Speeches of the Day,* vol. 51, no. 16 [Southhold, New York: City News Publishing Co., 1985].) Mr. Cox was addressing problems professional writers have when creative thoughts refuse to flow. I would like to use this thought in a different way. How do you as youth motivate a mind that seems to have little concern for your courses at school or limited interest in anything that leans toward work?

Self-motivation is an interesting study. We tend to want to repeat experiences that have been pleasurable or exciting. Satan, that old devil, is a genius in "motivating the clogged brain." He turns the brain on by thoughts of sex, pornography, dirty stories, gratification, and so on. Too many of our young people are unsuspectingly becoming addicted to unhealthy mental stimulation.

Sometimes even well-meaning teachers attempt to stretch the brain by using "sensational" stories. One educator said, "There is nothing wrong with making a good story better." That is not true. The truth will stand alone. I have made it a practice over the years to follow the Master's example of teaching. I use a lot of stories (parables). Occasionally someone will ask me if a story is true. I have always been grateful to be able to explain that the stories are accurate and honest. This does not mean that I do not use a fable, a legend, or a parable. I do. But I have always been very careful not to add to a story to improve it. Great stories do not have to be changed to be impressive.

Following are ways to motivate the clogged brain:

First, cultivate your receptiveness to the Holy Ghost. Have an understanding of the divine mission of the Holy Ghost. By the power of the Holy Ghost we may know the truth of all things. (See Moroni 10:6.) The Spirit is extremely sensitive. It abides only in clean and pure minds and hearts. It withdraws quickly and returns only after adjustments (repentance in some cases) take place. The Holy Ghost has access to all knowledge and can and does inspire men and women, youth and children, not only in religious pursuits but also in their daily activities. Many seemingly innocent acts cause its immediate withdrawal—the telling of a lie, stretching the truth, deceit, unwholesome thoughts, some music, ridicule, impatience, lack of performance, violation of the Word of Wisdom, and every unholy, unkind, evil, or selfish deed. On the other hand, what a blessing the Holy Ghost is to those who live worthy of it! On three memorable occasions I have been asked to give blessings to good, honest, righteous men who were in difficulty. We might not think it would be a righteous desire to ask God to bless us during time of personal difficulties not related to health. But other needs often are equally as important as a temporary health problem. I always give my children blessings as they return to school each fall.

The Holy Ghost is the greatest force in motivating the clogged brain. It will inspire, direct, teach, and guide anyone who is a member of the Church who lives worthy and seeks for a blessing. Tap into this high power line. Call constantly on the Lord and energy, knowledge, and wisdom will flow and unclog the brain.

Second, keep healthy and strong. When you are weary, tired, fatigued, or ill you do not think clearly. Keep yourself in good physical condition. Eat good, wholesome food in a well-balanced diet. Remember moderation in all things.

Sometime in your life you will be required to give energy beyond what you suppose is your limit. When that time comes, if you have prepared well you will be able to call on physical powers beyond what you would ever suppose.

Some years back a young man was missing on a mountain. A search party was organized in which I had the privilege of participating. On the third day he was missing, we started early in the morning before sunup and searched all day—to no avail. I found out later that his wonderful, noble, old father had been on the mountain and had searched for three days and three nights. He never left the mountain during those three days. To my knowledge, he never even slept. In due time they found the son, who was unharmed physically but under some unusual mental stress. Picture a man in his mid-sixties tramping and climbing through the hills for three days and nights. If he had been asked beforehand if he could do such a feat, he would have said no—but he did.

As a young produce supervisor for a major grocery store chain, I assisted in opening a new store in Cheyenne, Wyoming. Long hours of work were required in preparation for the opening, and in spite of our preparation I do not think anyone was ready for the volume of business we did that week. As nearly as I can remember, I worked about 120 hours in a one-week period. I was going to the store at 4:00 A.M. and working until midnight. The pace was terrific. We had a good strong crew but we were all giving more than we thought we could give.

Then, too, who will ever forget the valiant effort by the gymnast Shun Fujimoto during the 1976 Olympics? He broke a bone in his leg the day before the finals. It was x-rayed and put in a cast. The next day he showed up for the finals in his special event—without the weighty cast. As he dismounted from his routine on the still rings, he did a triple somersault and landed on his feet. He held his position for a moment, then collapsed in agony and pain. He won a gold medal. After the event someone said to him, "The pain must have been excruciating." He said, "It was terrible beyond belief, but now the pain is gone and I have a gold medal."

Physical and mental conditioning are necessary to unclog the brain and motivate it in the right direction. Few great successes come without tremendous effort.

Third, make it a habit to develop your mind, to hunger and thirst for great thoughts. Read good materials. Listen to classical and great music. Examine the discourses and writings of superior thinkers and intellects. Study the scriptures daily. The prophets always have a poetic-like style of speaking and teaching. If I recall correctly, President David O. McKay's favorite writings in the scriptures were 1 and 2 Peter. How was it that this fisherman called Peter, the chief of the Apostles, could appeal to this teacher, educator, and modern prophet of God? Go back and read 1 and 2 Peter and feel and respond to the spiritual eloquence.

Our prophet today and other members of the First Presidency and the Twelve have special teaching endowments. Their words flow like the crystal waters, like the verdant pastures, like gentle rains from heaven.

We can learn a great deal by examining the most brilliant contributions of good men of the past and great men in our own day.

Stretch your mind. Think with intensity. Elder Thomas S. Monson has stated that thinking is the hardest work we ever do. He is a superb example. He has an ability to remember facts, names, and places better than anyone else I have ever known.

In a recent talk he referred to a time when he was a young bishop. The Presiding Bishopric's Office had sent him the membership record of a member of the Church by mistake. He checked it out and returned the membership record. The amazing thing is that he still remembers the name of the family whose record only passed through his ward.

We have talked before about the addiction some youth and adults have to pornography. Sometimes the addiction is more severe and more profound than is that of those who are addicted to cigarettes, alcohol, or drugs. Mental addictions are on the mind constantly.

We know from experience and studies that the mind is at work constantly with only a few moments each day for rest. Like a river, a mind that is not disciplined will follow the course of least resistance, generally leading downward.

Television is a great blessing to humanity. All over the world people are being educated and exposed to other parts of the world. It can be a blessing and benefit to man, as the Church is proving. It can also be a great detriment if our lusts and desires for it are undisciplined and unmanaged. Be selective. There are times when good, wholesome entertainment is as important as a quest for valuable knowledge. To give the greatest spring and tension, the bow should not always be taut. There must be time for release, but that release should always be wholesome and positive, appealing to the higher nature in man.

Use your mind. Increase your mental capacity. Develop mental habits of selectivity that always lift and elevate to noble thoughts and actions. Good habits have a way of taking over when our brains seem clogged, and soon they have us thinking constructive thoughts.

Memorize something regularly. It is a good discipline for the mind and a mental reserve for a future need or opportunity. I have memorized much and it is always there for instant retrieval.

Fourth and finally, practice service, charity, and purity in your life. Making yourself available for service is a qualification of a believer. Service is seldom convenient but is always essential in our quest for eternal life. Service is sweetest when it comes without grumbling or complaint. Those who truly love the Lord seek every available opportunity to serve. They know that when they serve their fellowmen they are walking in the footsteps of the Master. There is no more rewarding path.

I recently gave a talk for which I did not have a title. As I stood up I stated: "If my talk had a title it would be something like this: 'I love this church and its leaders with all the heart and soul I have and with every particle of my being. I love to serve. I have always sought opportunities to go to the cannery, the welfare farm, home teaching, the hospital, the temple, and other places of service, and have loved it. It has not been a burden to have an assignment in the Church. The greatest trial of my membership was a short period when I did not have a calling. I love the Savior and have subscribed my total life in his service.' "

Well, of course, that is too lengthy a title for a talk, but as I said those words I had to halt momentarily to overcome the great swellings of emotion that I felt.

Remember, my friends, cultivate the power of the Holy Ghost in your total life. Remain strong and healthy in mind and body. Develop and increase your capacity to think and enrich your soul. And, finally, use that inspiration, that health and strength, and that alert and imaginative mind to "motivate the clogged brain." Serve your fellowmen. You will find the "treasure hidden in the field" and "the pearl of great price." You will come to know that these things are most precious—above all the diamonds, rubies, and gold, beyond any worldly success, and greater than any other achievement. Success is fast in fleeing. Service generates a continual flow of blessings. "Whatsoever ye sow, that shall ye also reap" is the law of the harvest (D&C 6:33). Sow wisely, my beloved associates, and reap blessings for eternity.

Learning from the Great Thinkers

Books, poetry, and music have always been very special in my life. It is evident from the speaking of the Brethren that they have an insatiable appetite for great thoughts and ideals, for beautiful music and poetry. You will find that much is learned as we stretch our minds in the directions great authors and composers lead us. Always remember that reading good literature is not drudgery. It is a stimulating, exciting, expanding, and rewarding experience.

I have made a feeble attempt to do some writing, including poetry. Rare is the person who does not have to labor diligently, writing and rewriting many times, before the effort is rewarded with something worthwhile. This does not suggest that we do not have moments of inspiration, but rather that even under inspiration great labor may be required to transfer thoughts from the mind to the paper.

There are great ideas that have a terrific influence on our thinking. An example is this short story by Damon Runyon. It is great not only for what it says but more important for its unwritten message.

> Doc Brackett didn't have black whiskers.
> Nonetheless, he was a fine man.

He doctored in Our Town for many years. He doctored more people than any other doctor in Our Town but made less money.

That was because Doc Brackett was always doctoring poor people, who had no money to pay.

He would get up in the middle of the coldest night and ride twenty miles to doctor a sick woman, or child, or to patch up some fellow who got hurt.

Everybody in Our Town knew Doc Brackett's office over Rice's clothing store. It was up a narrow flight of stairs. His office was always filled with people. A sign at the foot of the stairs said: Dr. Brackett, Office Upstairs.

Doc Brackett was a bachelor. He was once supposed to marry Miss Elvira Cromwell, the daughter of old Junius Cromwell, the banker, but on the day the wedding was supposed to take place Doc Brackett got a call to go out into the country and doctor a Mexican child. Miss Elvira got sore at him and called off the wedding. She said that a man who would think more of a Mexican child than of his wedding was no good. Many women in Our Town agreed with Miss Elvira Cromwell, but the parents of the Mexican child were very grateful to Doc Brackett when the child recovered.

For forty years, the lame, and the halt, and the blind of Our Town had climbed up and down the stairs to Doc Brackett's office.

He never turned away anybody.

Some said Doc Brackett was a loose character, because he liked to drink whisky and play poker in the back rooms of saloons.

But he lived to be seventy years old, and then one day he keeled over on the sofa in his office and died. By this time his black hair had turned white.

Doc Brackett had one of the biggest funerals ever seen in Our Town. Everybody went to pay their last respects when he was laid out in Gruber's undertaking parlors. He was buried in Riverview Cemetery.

There was talk of raising money to put a nice tombstone on Doc Brackett's grave as a memorial. The talk got as far as arguing about what should be carved on the stone about him. Some thought poetry would be very nice.

Doc Brackett hated poetry.

The matter dragged along and nothing whatever was done.

Then one day George Gruber, the undertaker, said that Doc Brackett's memorial was already over his grave, with an epitaph and all. George Gruber said the Mexican parents of the child Doc Brackett saved years ago had worried about him having no tombstone.

They had no money themselves, so they took the sign from the foot of the stairs at Doc Brackett's office and stuck it over his grave. It read: Dr. Brackett, Office Upstairs. ("Doc Brackett," in *One Thousand Inspirational Things,* comp. Audrey Stone Morris [New York: The Spencer Press, Inc., 1948], pp. 38–39.)

A sweet story like this elevates and lifts the soul and teaches the quiet message that somehow the majority of the people seem to sense what is right. They somehow know and do the right thing. They are not deceived by gossip, rumors, or lies.

Henry Drummond in *The Greatest Thing in the World* cites this little verse:

> I lived for myself, I thought for
>   myself,
> For myself, and none beside—
> Just as if Jesus had never lived,
> As if He had never died.
> (*The Greatest Thing in the World*
> [London and Glasgow: Collins], p. 56.)

This little verse bends our thinking in a different direction than we are normally wont to think. I took occasion to write a poem sometime ago, and later was interested to see that some of my thoughts crossed over his. I entitled it, "Who Follows in the Steps He Trod":

> I met a man the other day
>   Who faced endless problems on his way.
> His heart was sad, all hope was gone,
>   He walked in night from dark to dawn.
> The emptiness that ruled his life
>   Remained through all his toil and strife.
> The barren deserts seemed less bleak
>   Than the life he lived from week to week.
>
> The years were multiplied to ten—
>   I met this selfsame man again.
> This time he seemed a different soul,
>   In every way he had control.
> His step was light, his heart was gay,
>   He always had kind words to say.
> He blessed the lives of all he met,
>   Not one escaped his cast-out net.

The stranger was a welcome friend—
    Each broken heart he set to mend.
Nor forgot he still the orphan boy,
    Or the lonely widow who felt no joy.
No heartsick soul escaped his glance,
    Nor did he leave their case to chance.
His worldly wealth he soon spread thin;
    No troubled soul he took not in.

And so from dawn to dusk he shared—
    All who knew him said he cared.
This empty life we see thus changed,
    Seemed almost by his God arranged.
And true it is and ever so,
    The Master's touch on all below,
Who follow in the steps he trod,
    Will turn the hearts of men to God.

Julian Dyke, a great professional Scouter for the Boy Scouts of America, shared a story with the Young Men's general board during a visit to Salt Lake City.

Vice-President Calvin Coolidge had just become President due to the death of President Warren G. Harding. Since Mrs. Harding was still living in the White House, the Coolidges remained in the third-floor suite in the Willard Hotel where they had lived during the Vice-Presidency. In the middle of the night the new President awoke to see an intruder going through his clothes. He watched as the thief removed a wallet and unhooked a watch chain. So, in the darkness, Coolidge calmly spoke up and said, "About the watch, I wish you wouldn't take that."

The startled man, gaining his voice, asked, "Why?" Coolidge answered, "I don't mean the watch and chain, only the charm. I'm very fond of that charm. It means a great deal to me. Take it near the window and read what is engraved on the back of it."

And the burglar read: "Presented to Calvin Coolidge, Speaker of the House, by the Massachusetts General Court."

Then the amazed burglar asked, "Are you President Coolidge?"

"Yes, I am, and I don't want you to take that charm." Then Coolidge said to him, "Why, son, are you doing this?"

"Mr. President, my friend and I came down from college to have a vacation in Washington. We spent all our money, and haven't got enough to pay our hotel bill and get back to the campus. If you don't mind, I'll just take the wallet."

Well, Coolidge was an old-fashioned Yankee and he knew there was eighty dollars in the wallet. So he said: "How much will it take to pay your hotel bill and get you and your friend back to the campus? Sit down and let's talk this over."

Coolidge added up the room rate and two rail tickets back to the campus. It came to thirty-two dollars. Of course, this was a long while ago, before inflation. Coolidge continued, "I'll give you the thirty-two dollars as a loan, and I expect you to pay me back."

"Thank you, Mr. President," said the astonished young man.

President Coolidge then told the intruder that there probably was a secret service agent patroling the hotel corridor, and he had better go back out the window, along the ledge, the way he came in. And as the thief was on the way out the President said to him: "Son, you're a nice boy. You are better than you are acting. You are starting down the wrong road. Just remember who you are." The boy went out through the window. The President went back to bed.

Later the President confided this strange incident to two friends, Judge Walter L. Stevens, the family lawyer, and Frank MacCarthy, a free-lance writer and photographer.

The President pledged MacCarthy to silence and never told him the intruder's name. As the twenty-fifth anniversary of the event approached, fifteen years after Coolidge's death, MacCarthy, then working for the Springfield Union, asked Mrs. Coolidge to let him use the story.

She declined, saying, "There is already too much publicity given to acts of vandalism and violence."

MacCarthy honored her request, asking only that she review the story for accuracy and allow him to use it after her death.

Mrs. Coolidge died July 8, 1957, and MacCarthy died less than four months later without publishing the article.

MacCarthy had shared the story with another reporter, Richard C. Garvey, when they worked together. Because all reasons for secrecy had now vanished, this report was reconstructed from MacCarthy's article by Garvey and published in the Los Angeles Times.

The story had a happy ending, for the late President's notes show that the young man repaid the thirty-two-dollar loan in full.

The point is that President Coolidge handled that young man in his crisis, not like an officer of the law, which he was sworn to be, but like a father or friend. He convinced the boy that he was greater than he was acting. (From "There Is Something Great in You," by Norman Vincent Peale, published in *PLUS: The Magazine of Positive Thinking*, Box FCL, Pawling, New York 12564.)

You have to search for stories like this. We seldom just stumble across them. Missionaries who served in my mission asked me to list great books I have read so that they might also consider reading them. Of course such a list would never be all-inclusive; and, even as I responded to their questions and supplied a list, I realized it was very limited. Of the books that have influenced my life, many were read in my younger years. I could list many more from recent years, but I believe this first list would be those I would suggest to you, my young friends. Every one broadened my vision and expanded my soul. You may want to select from this list the books you feel would interest you.

> *Les Miserables* by Victor Hugo
> *Ben Hur* by General Lew Wallace
> *The Hunchback of Notre Dame* by Victor Hugo
> *Call of the Wild* by Jack London
> *Moby Dick* by Herman Melville
> *Mutiny on the Bounty* by Charles Nordhoff and James Norman Hall
> *Northwest Passage* and other books by Kenneth Roberts
> *David Copperfield* by Charles Dickens
> *The Agony and the Ecstasy* by Irving Stone
> *Uncle Tom's Cabin* by Harriett Beecher Stowe
> *The Robe, The Big Fisherman,* and *The Magnificent Obsession*
>   by Lloyd Douglas
> *Helen Keller* by Helen Keller
> *Jonathan Livingston Seagull* by Richard Bach
> *The Clowns of God* by Morris West
> *Happy Homes and the Hearts That Make Them* by Samuel Smiles
> *The Pearl* by John E. Steinbeck
> *Treasure Island* by Robert Louis Stevenson
> *The Adventures of Tom Sawyer* and *Adventures of Huckleberry Finn*
>   by Mark Twain
> *The Go-Getter* by Peter B. Kyne
> *The Greatest Salesman in the World* by Og Mandino
> *The Miracle of Personality* by Lewis Fischer
> *Acres of Diamonds* by Russell Conwell
> *Shakespeare's Works* by Shakespeare
> *How to Win Friends and Influence People* by Dale Carnegie
> *Dynamic Leadership* by Lynn Fluckiger
> Louis L'Amour's books are entertaining, clean Westerns

Then, of course, there is the great list of books authored by the Brethren. I have loved reading them, especially those by the First Presidency and the Twelve. These are the men whom I love and admire most, and I want to know what they think. Also, there are other wonderful Church authors who are not General Authorities but have great talent and insight and who have sufficient time to make in-depth studies on particular subjects.

Always be reading something good. Find your special interest and then good books will hold you like a giant magnet. You will hardly be able to lay them down. Life will expand. You can journey, be involved in adventure, experience emotions, and have experiences that could not seem more real. Read every day a few minutes or longer, but read daily. Always read the scriptures daily. Read them along with whatever else you may read. This will keep your focus on the right things. Remember, there are valuable things to learn from great thinkers.

Discipline yourself to always accommodate the things which matter most. Our spiritual and intellectual development is imperative.

Becoming a Friend

One of the basic human desires is to have true friends. We have often heard that "to have a friend, you must be one." This is true. You will find in life that true friendships are very precious. We have numerous companions, associates, and fellow workers, but only a handful of true friends. Sometimes we refer to people as friends when indeed they are not.

The scriptural reference to friends gives us insight into the Lord's understanding of friends. The Lord spoke to Moses "as a man speaketh unto his friend" (Exodus 33:11). In John we read, "Greater love hath no man than this, that he lay down his life for his friends." Then he continues, "Ye are my friends." This type of sacrifice has somehow rung down through the centuries to represent the bond that exists between friends.

Seek to have true friends. They are a comfort in time of sorrow, stress, or sickness. They share in your joy in times of accomplishment and success. They counsel you wisely when you need another opinion you can trust. A true friend is not fickle, clambering from one association to another. A true friend will always be there in time of need. Remember again, you must be a true friend with no expectation of reward even though the benefits will come. Friendships built on the basis of "What's in it for me?" are not constructed on a true foundation.

Sometime ago on a Monday (a day which General Authorities try to spend with their families) I was alone with my wife. During a sweet talk we were having I said to her, "Merlene, who is your very dearest friend on the earth?" It took some courage to ask the question. I wanted her to say that I was; but I am not home very often and my hours are long. She has learned to fill her life with meaningful activities in service and with family. She is a very well adjusted woman. She has many special "friends" in the true sense of the word, some with whom she is very close. She looked at me for a long moment, then tears began to glisten in her eyes and she said: "You are my very dearest friend in this world. You are not home often and quite often you are away when I need you, but you are my dearest friend." I was touched.

As you date, go out with people who could be dear friends. Our daughter, Jill, who is in college, sat and visited with me about some concerns. As we talked, the subject changed to a need for friends. I said to her: "Jill, your mother is the very dearest friend you have; please work on keeping that relationship. One time one of your brothers had a disagreement with his mother and I told him the same thing. His mother is the best friend he has."

Friends think about, pray about, care about, and are concerned about you. My wife has been a sweet friend to many people and she has a lot of choice friends.

The Royal Bank of America publishes a bimonthly newsletter. They have included several statements in an article that I believe ought to be considered:

> It should not take a crisis to test the strength of a friendship, because "the one who will be found capable of great acts of love is ever the one who is doing considerate small ones." As F. W. Robertson put it, "Home, marriage, families, church, school and other settings are places where small loving deeds can be done that cement friendships."

The article goes on to state that friendships are often forged in the crucible of mutual adversity."

Missionary companions oftentimes become lifelong friends. They have knelt together and pleaded with the Lord on behalf of a family. Theirs is a union, a companionship, of knocking on many doors, everlastingly searching for the honest in heart. I have known missionaries who silently wept together as they watched converts being baptized. At Christmas, in a little, neat, clean apartment far away from home, a humble tree and a meager meal is shared with love between two true friends. Yet there is a third involved, for the Lord said, "Where two or three are gathered together in my name, there am I in the midst of them" (Matthew 18:20).

Our son Ron became very close to his first missionary companion, Elder Joseph Call. I remember the name because we felt so blessed that our son would have a great, first missionary companion. Joseph Call was great. At the first Christmas, Elder Call's package did not arrive in time, due to the mail delays. Ron shared his Christmas gifts with Elder Call. He invited Elder Call to take any Christmas package. Elder Call took the smallest one. Ron said, "No, take one of these big, beautiful packages." They discussed it for some time until Ron finally persuaded Elder Call to take a larger gift.

The small gift was a ruby ring that we had sent to our son for that Christmas. It was more valuable than all the other gifts together. Knowing Ron, if Elder Call had kept the small gift and opened it, he would have been excited that Elder Call received such a "neat" gift. On the other hand, knowing what Ron has shared with me about Elder Call, I am sure he would have insisted that Ron take it back.

True friends seem to care more about others than they do about themselves and are often amazingly selfless in their relationships with their friends.

When my wife, Merlene, and I were growing up, I liked her and wanted to date her. We lived in the same ward. She was going with a good friend in our priests quorum. I did not ask her out on a date until they broke up. He was too good a friend for me to move into his territory.

Sometimes friends are not always the same age. My older brother had a Scoutmaster, Don Stout, who is one of the finest men I have met. Don Stout was also our Sunday School teacher. We got to know him well. We all felt that he was a friend. He was drafted into the Army during the Second World War. Many of us wrote to him and have been in touch with him over the years. He is a few years older than we are but he is as close a friend as a boy will ever find. The years did not make any difference in the friendship.

Merlene served at one time as the president of the Young Women in the Valley View Sixth Ward. The bishop's daughter, Pat Pehrson, was one of the young women. My wife is a dozen or so years older than she is, yet a friendship bloomed that is more precious today than it was over twenty years ago. I believe Pat was only fourteen at the time. This year they attended Education Week at BYU together. Friendship is true when it endures. Everyone has weaknesses and a true friend accepts those weaknesses of the other party and still values all the best and good.

Ralph Waldo Emerson said, "The friends we are likely to cherish most are the ones with whom we have travelled long and far over the rough patches of life along with the smooth." On the essence of friendship he states, "To feel and say of another, I need never meet, or speak, or write to him; we need not reinforce ourselves and send tokens of remembrance; I rely on him as on myself."

Through the years I have observed that some of the people I would most dearly like to associate with, who are truly friends, who I would entrust with anything are seldom in contact. Our work takes us in different directions. Robert Ferguson and Dale Newbold were friends when I grew up. It is interesting that we have now served on the Young Men's general board together. Terry Nofsinger was a Scout in my troop when I served as Scoutmaster. He also serves with us. A friend of mine, Neil Schmitt, was an associate in business and the Church and is as dear to me today as he was years ago.

I have several nonmember friends that I love and respect. J. L. Scott, who was the chief executive officer of Albertson's when I worked for them, is one of them. When I was called to be a General Authority, I called his secretary to make an appointment and to tell him of my resignation from the company. His secretary checked with him and then called back and said, "He will come to your office." I told her that I could not consider it and asked her to tell me what time he had arranged to come. I thought I would go over to his office a few minutes before that. She told me the time, but before I got to his office he came to mine. He came in, shut the door, and sat down. We visited as though he had all the time in the world. To this day I prize his friendship and love him even though we only occasionally cross paths.

Another man, Hugh Burnett, hired me when I was fifteen. He was not married and he lived with and took care of his mother. Hugh is not a member of the Church but has always been a fine human being. He had an ability to motivate and train me in a way that I am just beginning to understand. I first went to work in the produce department. Hugh asked me to buy a pocket knife with which I could trim produce. Months passed and he had asked me at least a dozen times to buy a knife. He did not fire me; he even seemed to understand. I took almost every penny I made and gave it to my mother. There was nothing left with which to buy a knife. I wanted to buy one, in the worst way, but I chose to give the money to Mom instead. Hugh eventually arranged to have a knife given to me by one of our suppliers. Hugh was always wonderful with people. He loved children, he was kind to customers, the employees liked him, and I thought the world of him. Many times when he was on the phone, I heard him say as I walked past, "I have a young man working with me who is the finest I have ever had." He complimented me constantly and seldom criticized me, although I know I needed it at times. Hugh was a good worker, a thoughtful son, an excellent produce man, and the kind of friend and trainer every young man needs.

Although I have not seen him in years, his influence and friendship to a young man have been very important.

"A Middle Eastern Proverb defines a friend as 'one who gives you warning.' There may be times when it is your bounden duty to call attention to the potential folly of a friend's act. We would not, after all, stand by in silence and watch a friend suffer an injury from a third party without intervening. By the same token, we should not stand by and watch a friend injure him or herself." (Samuel Smiles, *Happy Homes and the Hearts That Make Them* [Chicago: U.S. Publishing House, 1882].)

Sometimes our youth have misplaced loyalty and a misunderstanding about friendship. I know a young man who is "strung out" on drugs. He has been for several years. It has taken a great toll in his life. His countenance is dull, his energy level is low, he is not happy, and he has cost his parents tens of thousands of dollars. He buys cocaine on the street from a pusher. This young man protects the cocaine pusher and will not divulge his name even though the pusher may be the worst enemy he has. Those who push filth and drugs that reach into the lives of people and destroy them will be held accountable before the high courts of God. In a way, they will be partially responsible for the deaths of many who have become addicted and have either committed suicide or accidentally taken an overdose. What a tragedy that loyalty and friendship are misused and not understood.

A true friend will do what needs to be done even when he feels that the friendship will be impaired. I know some young people who have "friends" who are on drugs or who may be homosexuals, but they will not tell the bishop, because that "would not be loyal to a friend." Actually keeping quiet at such a time is the greatest disservice to any friendship. We need to do what is necessary to save them even at the risk of friendship. Also, we need to have more loyalty to the Church and to our leaders than we do to those who transgress. Those who transgress lose the Spirit. They are not guided by the Spirit. They lose wisdom and judgment, and yet they have strong opinions of what the Church should do for the drug addict and for the homosexual. The Lord has his program for those who will repent.

Beware of those who try to appeal to their victim's ("friend's") vanity by feigning admiration and affection. We need to "be advised that all flatterers live at the expense of those who listen to them" (Smiles, *Happy Homes*).

Remember, "in any case, there can be no authentic friendship where one party contrives to get more out of it than the other. In a real friendship, the less fortunate party would be just as forthcoming if the roles were reversed." (Smiles, *Happy Homes*.)

As we go through this exciting experience of life, we must make new friends from our associates, else we soon find ourselves alone.

The Earl of Clarendon listed the qualifications for being a friend as "the skill and observation of the best physician, the vigilance and diligence of the best nurse, the tenderness and patience of the best mother." And, Jeremy Taylor, a bishop, was if anything more demanding in his description: "the greatest love, the greatest usefulness, the most open communication, the noblest sufferings, the severest truth, the heartiest counsel, and the greatest union of minds of which brave men and women are capable."

In conclusion, we have an opportunity to select friends from the finest people who walk the earth. I have heard the Brethren often speak about the unity in the First Presidency and the Twelve. These marvelous, great leaders are strong willed, they have superior and enlightened minds, and they are results-oriented. And yet there is a friendship, a brotherhood, a mutual respect that is dearer than life.

Becoming a friend to people of high quality and with Christ-like ways can bring great satisfaction. Such friendships will extend into eternity.

Friendships are best when they are based on mutual trust and genuine interest with a caring heart. Seek good friends—those who excite, lift, and buoy us up; those who are true to the faith, trust in God, and walk in obedience. Life will be constantly an enriching experience as we develop wholesome friendships.

My young friends, go out and be a friend to someone in desperate need. The Master taught, "Inasmuch as ye have done it unto one of the least of these my brethren, ye have done it unto me" (Matthew 25:40).

Flogging Theagenes

Let me bring you an ancient story:

What decision sequence or turn of fate led historians to record the story of Theagenes, a Greek athlete of 500 B.C., will, I suppose, remain a mystery and continue to remind us that history is a human construction and not a dry collection of events devoid of the historian's emotions, interests, and values. That such a remote frame of history could be found 2500 years later in the modest library of LSU-Shreveport is one of those pleasant intellectual wonders that fuels my curiosity each time I cross the threshold of a university library.

A citizen of Thasus, Theagenes was a formidable athlete who won more than 1400 prizes in the games of those days. On his death, admirers erected a statue in his honor. Apparently in angry jealousy, one of his detractors came each evening to flog the statue of Theagenes. The nightly flogging continued, according to the ancient chronicles, until one evening the statue of Theagenes avenged itself by falling upon the author of the lash, killing him.

Here is an ancient story with modern import, the tragic story of a talent throwing itself against the achievement and record of another, unable and unwilling to find a more constructive outlet than the flogging of a cold and sterile marker. How many unfortunate colleagues have you and I seen flogging the statue of Theagenes— expending precious energy and talent attacking the personality, the achievements, the record of others. (E. Grady Bogue, "The Flogging of Theagenes: A Poverty of Leadership Vision," in *Vital Speeches of the Day* [Southold, New York: City News Publishing Co.], p. 597.)

One of the signs of the true church is the constant persecution it faces. Yet the Church truly is the only authorized agency to function on behalf of the Lord Jesus Christ. It was true in the days when the Master lived on the earth, it was true after his crucifixion, and it will be true in the future. Remember, my young friends, "pearls do not dissolve in mire" (Victor Hugo, *Les Miserables*, trans. Charles E. Wilbour [Random House, 1862]).

In Joseph's personal testimony he declared:

> However, it was nevertheless a fact that I had beheld a vision. I have thought since, that I felt much like Paul, when he made his defense before King Agrippa, and related the account of the vision he had when he saw a light, and heard a voice; but still there were but few who believed him; some said he was dishonest, others said he was mad; and he was ridiculed and reviled. But all this did not destroy the reality of his vision. He had seen a vision, he knew he had, and all the persecution under heaven could not make it otherwise; and though they should persecute him unto death, yet he knew, and would know to his latest breath, that he had both seen a light and heard a voice speaking unto him, and all the world could not make him think or believe otherwise.
>
> So it was with me. I had actually seen a light, and in the midst of that light I saw two Personages, and they did in reality speak to me; and though I was hated and persecuted for saying that I had seen a vision, yet it was true; and while they were persecuting me, reviling me, and speaking all manner of evil against me falsely for so saying, I was led to say in my heart: Why persecute me for telling the truth? I have actually seen a vision; and who am I that I can withstand God, or why does the world think to make me deny what I have actually seen? For I had seen a vision; I knew it, and I knew that God knew it, and I could not deny it, neither dared I do it; at least I knew that by so doing I would offend God, and come under condemnation. (Joseph Smith—History 1:24–25.)

There is a simple test that one can apply whenever frustration or confusion comes in a gospel setting. Go back to the very basic testimony of the Church. Everything pivots on the validity and authenticity of the Book of Mormon. No honest-in-heart member of the Church will ever be deceived if he will go back and read the Book of Mormon—praying, pondering, having faith in Christ.

Every page will be a witness that the book is true and all the persecution and satanic forces combined can never change that.

My young friends, I would rather die than deny my testimony of the Book of Mormon. With God as my witness, I testify that it is true. Enemies of the Church, religionists, pastors, preachers, and intellectuals could line up four abreast from San Francisco to Salt Lake City, and attempt to prove that Joseph Smith was not a Prophet and that the Book of Mormon is not true. And, when the last one had passed, I would know with everything in my soul that The Church of Jesus Christ of Latter-day Saints is the only true and living church of our Lord and Savior on the earth.

I cannot imagine what my life would be like without the influence and vicarious association I have had with the prophets in the Book of Mormon throughout my life.

They include Nephi, this "large in stature," pure, holy, totally obedient son of Lehi and his brother Jacob, who had "seen his Redeemer." King Benjamin, the venerable old Saint who delivered what might be the second greatest discourse ever, is among them. His son Mosiah and Mosiah's sons, who spent fourteen years preaching to the Lamanites, are also included. I love Abinadi, Alma and his sons, Mormon, Moroni, and the brother of Jared.

I have received such a powerful witness of the Book of Mormon, I fear that I would blaspheme to ever deny it. I know it is true.

You may not be able to argue as intellectually and as influentially as others may, but they cannot persuade you away from this church as long as you have a testimony of the Book of Mormon. When those who would persuade you away from your beliefs finish their statements, you say this: "I may not understand all you have said. I do not have the skill to refute your arguments, and I may never convince you differently, but I bear a sacred and solemn testimony that I know the Book of Mormon is true. I promise you that you also can absolutely know that it is true." Then refer them to Moroni 10:4 and encourage them to put it to the test.

A lady missionary talked to me at a zone conference. She told me that her father wrote to her every single week. He had been excommunicated and was sending her anti-Mormon materials. He pleaded with her to leave her mission, to stop wasting her time, and to return home. She said: "I love my father and I am becoming confused. I want to stay on my mission, but what can I do and what can I say to my father."

I asked her, "Do you mind if I wait and answer this question during my talk because all the missionaries should hear my answer?" She thought that would be good.

During my talk I referred to her question and then I said, "This is how I would suggest she respond to her father."

Dear Dad,

I love you. You are my father, but please do not send me any more anti-Mormon materials. I will not read them. I am not going to come home till my mission here is finished; and I know the Church is true. When you have something better than what I have, I will listen to you, but don't try to destroy what I have without replacing it with something better.

Give me something better than a church with a living prophet and Twelve Apostles, something better than temples and men with sealing powers who can seal a family together for time and eternity. Give me something better than a church that does genealogical research so that every soul that would ever inhabit this earth could have an opportunity to hear the gospel and have vicarious work performed in the temple. Show me another church that sends thirty thousand missionaries at their own expense to share the gospel of Jesus Christ. Expose me to any organization in the world that has a better program for providing for the poor, the sick, and the afflicted.

Share with me a church that calls the elders to administer to the sick and where miracles result as often as in my church. Show me something better than the blessings that come from payment of tithing, living of the Word of Wisdom, family home evening, family prayers, scripture reading, the opportunity to serve, and scripture from the Lord in our day and our time.

Do you know of a better organization for the youth than our church has, better than the Primary for children, a better organization for the sisters than Relief Society—and all of this without a paid ministry.

I love you and I pray for your welfare. You are wrong. The Church of Jesus Christ of Latter-day Saints is true. I know it.

Love,

———————————

Elder Boyd K. Packer, talking about apostates in a baccalaure-
ate address given several years ago at Utah State University, said,
"They leave the Church but they cannot leave it alone." That is
prophecy. On another occasion he talked about an apostate and
said, "Within a short period of time that person will be arrested
for civil disobedience." Within two months a picture and article
in the paper verified his prophetic comment.

A poem that gives cause for reflection is a good reminder to all
of us:

Which Are You?

> I watched them tearing a building down,
> A gang of men in a busy town.
> With a ho-heave-ho and a lusty yell,
> They swung the beams and the side walls fell.
>
> I asked the foreman, "Are these men skilled,
> The kind you'd hire were you to build?"
> He laughed and said, "Why, no indeed!
> Just common laborers are all I need.
> They can easily wreck in a day or two
> What builders have taken years to do."
>
> And I thought to myself as I went my way:
> "What part in the game of life do I play?
> Am I a builder who works with care,
> Measuring life by the rule and the square?
> Am I shaping my deeds to a well-made plan,
> Patiently doing the best I can?
> Or am I a wrecker who walks the town,
> Content with the labor of tearing down?"
>   —Authorship Unknown

There are wreckers who walk city streets destroying, breaking,
and tearing down, but they will reap as they sow.

Remember, my young friends, there are two things that Satan
can never bring about or cause to happen—peace and love
(charity). He is the author of lies, hate, deceit, evil, filth, darkness,
and corruption.

Only our God, when we abide in his commandments, can bring us peace.

In the prayer offered at the dedication of the Kirtland Temple, Joseph Smith prayed these inspired words. (The prayer was revealed to Joseph because it would become a model for all temple dedicatory prayers.)

That no weapon formed against them shall prosper; that he who diggeth a pit for them shall fall into the same himself;

That no combination of wickedness shall have power to rise up and prevail over thy people upon whom thy name shall be put in this house;

And if any people shall rise against this people, that thine anger be kindled against them;

And if they shall smite this people thou wilt smite them; thou wilt fight for thy people as thou didst in the day of battle, that they may be delivered from the hands of all their enemies.

We ask thee, Holy Father, to confound, and astonish, and to bring to shame and confusion, all those who have spread lying reports abroad, over the world, against thy servant or servants, if they will not repent, when the everlasting gospel shall be proclaimed in their ears. (D&C 109:25–29.)

Also, in section 121 the Lord declared:

And they who do charge thee with transgression, their hope shall be blasted, and their prospects shall melt away as the hoar frost melteth before the burning rays of the rising sun;

And also that God hath set his hand and seal to change the times and seasons and to blind their minds, that they may not understand his marvelous workings; that he may prove them also and take them in their own craftiness;

Also because their hearts are corrupted, and the things which they are willing to bring upon others, and love to have others suffer, may come upon themselves to the very uttermost;

That they may be disappointed also, and their hopes may be cut off;

And not many years hence, that they and their posterity shall be swept from under heaven, saith God, that not one of them is left to stand by the wall.

Cursed are all those that shall lift up the heel against mine anointed, saith the Lord, and cry they have sinned when they have not sinned before me, saith the Lord, but have done that which was meet in mine eyes, and which I commanded them.

But those who cry transgression do it because they are the servants of sin, and are the children of disobedience themselves.

And those who swear falsely against my servants, that they might bring them into bondage and death—Wo unto them; because they have offended my little ones they shall be severed from the ordinances of mine house.

Their basket shall not be full, their houses and their barns shall perish, and they themselves shall be despised by those that flattered them. (D&C 121:11–20.)

There are many more statements about those who attempt to frustrate this work, but who will never succeed.

One major church allocated $1 million to combat the missionary program of the Church. On the other hand, The Church of Jesus Christ of Latter-day Saints (members in the United States and Canada) fasted on a special Sunday and contributed an offering of over $6 million to aid our Father's children in Ethiopia and other parts of Africa. Which of these two acts is Christian? Which do you suppose would be an affront to all that Christianity represents?

Remember that "by their fruits ye shall know them" (Matthew 7:20).

Flogging Theagenes is one thing. Exerting effort to destroy wholesome and helpful efforts to bring people to Christ is quite another. The old hymn that asks "Who's on the Lord's Side, Who?" poses a question we might ask of ourselves when someone starts criticizing the Church or its leaders. Let us make certain that we are on the side of the Lord.

PART TWO

PURIFY YOUR LIFE

A Treasure Beyond Price

At the age of sixteen I worked in a supermarket in the produce department. We had a little, old, crippled man by the name of "Pops" who would come in and work. He would clean up the back room and stack all the boxes in exchange for the privilege of taking overripe or partially spoiled fruit and vegetables. He was about seventy-five years old, with one leg shorter than the other. Despite having a six-inch lift on his left leg, he had a severe limp. He was a good man and all of us at the store enjoyed having him around. He visited the store two or three times a week. We had another man who worked part-time in the produce department but who was also the full-time sign painter for the company. His name was Clarence Kelch. I believe Clarence was a convert to the Church. He had made an intense study of the gospel and was well founded in an understanding of the doctrine.

Pops was a member of the Reorganized Church. He loved the Book of Mormon and he loved to talk about the Prophet Joseph. We would talk and listen while we worked in the back room together. One day Pops was coming on pretty strong about The Church of Jesus Christ of Latter-day Saints not being true. He used several points of view as he attempted to prove that his church was the true church.

Clarence Kelch said to him, "Who is the founder of your church?" He responded, "The Prophet Joseph Smith." Clarence Kelch said, "The founder of our church is the Lord Jesus Christ." I remember the thrill in my soul as a young man when I heard that truth spoken. It was always exciting and stimulating to listen to intelligent, well-read men talk about the scriptures.

Years later, after I was married, I was the co-manager of the produce department in the largest store in the chain. We had eight full-time employees and six part-time employees in the produce department. A former missionary and a great young man, Darrell Richards, came to work during the summer months for several years. He was a scripturalist. The store opened at 9:00 A.M. I would start work about 5:30 A.M. and the rest of the early crew came on at 6:00 A.M.

Darrell will never know the great influence he had on those of us who worked with him. He would quote scriptures and ask us for the reference. At first we did not do very well. I would go home at night and memorize a scripture and go back the next day and quote it and question him about the reference. It became an exciting scriptural duel. I memorized many scriptures during that period of my life. I read all the standard works and became acquainted with those scriptures that are used most by the missionaries. We even had one or two scriptures painted on a sign which we hung on the wall. One of those was: "There hath no temptation taken you but such as is common to man: but God is faithful, who will not suffer you to be tempted above that ye are able; but will with the temptation also make a way to escape, that ye may be able to bear it" (1 Corinthians 10:13).

As I thought back on that experience, it was a great time in my life. Darrell had an influence on a lot of young men, many of whom were in their teens. We all grew and learned to find excitement in the scriptures. It was during that time that I memorized the entire Sermon on the Mount from Matthew.

Studying the scriptures—the doctrines, prophecies, and revelations—can be a thrilling spiritual adventure.

Not too long ago I took my youngest son outside for a one-on-one talk. It was early evening and still light. I had him mark several scriptures about the Godhead. I explained to him the various concepts of other churches regarding the Godhead and then we read and marked his scriptures. We discussed what it meant to be created in the image of God and the three separate manifestations of the three members of the Godhead when Stephen looked up steadfastly into heaven, filled with the Holy Ghost, and he saw the glory of God and Jesus standing on his right hand. We read the account in chapter 24 of Luke in which the resurrected Lord appeared to the ten disciples. We read and marked other scriptures; then I said to him: "Paul, in addition to the things we have read, we have an additional witness; the Prophet Joseph Smith actually saw God the Eternal Father and his only Begotten Son Jesus Christ. These beings stood above him in the air and conversed with him. Joseph Smith knew more about the bodies of our Heavenly Father and Jesus Christ than all those engaged in leading other religious groups, because he had just seen them."

As we talked, Paul said, "Dad, I don't want to hurt your feelings but have you ever wondered whether the Church is really true?" I told him that I had as a young man. I explained that I had received a testimony by simply reading the Book of Mormon and by praying and pondering over what I had read.

My young friends, one of the most stimulating and exciting experiences of life is reading and studying the scriptures.

Faithfully read the Book of Mormon even if you have read it before. Read it over and over again. Study it and let its teachings become a vital part of your life.

The Book of Mormon is a thrilling study. I love it. Try to imagine what this church would be like without the Book of Mormon. Suppose we had never heard of Lehi, Nephi, Jacob, Enos, King Benjamin, the Almas, Helaman, Captain Moroni, the other Nephis, the Brother of Jared, Mormon, and Moroni. Life to me would be empty! I would not sell the precious jewels of knowledge I have obtained from reading the Book of Mormon for a million dollars or ten times that amount. I would rather die than deny my testimony of the truthfulness of the Book of Mormon. To me every page is a treasure beyond price.

On Saturday, April 6, 1963, Elder Spencer W. Kimball, then of
the Council of the Twelve, spoke at general conference. He said
this:

> May I tell you of a great adventure? As I traveled to a weekend
> assignment, I took with me an unusual book which was my constant
> companion. I could lay it down only to sleep, eat, and change trains.
> It fascinated me, captivated me, and held me spellbound with its
> irresistible charm and engaging interest. I have read it many times.
>
> As I finished it, I closed the book and sat back, absorbed as I
> relived its contents. Its pages held me, bound me, and my eyes were
> riveted to them. I knew the book was factual, but as has been said,
> "Truth is stranger than fiction."
>
> I am constrained to speak to you of it today. It is a story of cour-
> age, faith, and fortitude, of perseverance, sacrifice, and super-human
> accomplishments, of intrigue, of revenge, of disaster, of war, murder,
> and rapine, of idolatry, and of cannibalism, of miracles, visions, and
> manifestations, of prophecies and their fulfillment.
>
> I found in it life at its best and at its worst, in ever-changing pat-
> terns. I hardly recovered from one great crisis until another engulfed
> me.
>
> Across the stage of this drama of life through the ages, marched
> actors in exotic, colorful costumes from the blood-painted nudity of
> the warrior to the lavish, ornamented pageantry of royal courts—
> some actors loathsome and degraded, others so near perfection that
> they conversed with angels and with God. There are the sowers and
> the reapers, the artisans, the engineers, the traders, and the toilers,
> the rake in his debauchery, the alcoholic with his liquor, the pervert
> rotting in his sex, the warrior in his armor, the missionary on his
> knees.
>
> This dramatic story is one of the greatest ever played by man. The
> noted tragedians fumble their lines. It is played "on location" with
> no false fronts for scenery. It is a fast-moving story of total life, of
> opposing ideologies, of monarchies and judgeships and moboc-
> racies. Its scenes carry the reader across oceans and continents. It
> promises to tell of the "last days of God," but instead records the
> "last days of populous peoples" and the triumph of God. Class dis-
> tinction is there with its ugliness, race prejudice with its hatefulness,
> multiplicity of creeds with their bitter conflicts. (Conference Report,
> April 1963, pp. 62–63. Copyright by The Church of Jesus Christ of
> Latter-day Saints. Used by permission.)

Of course, he is speaking of the Book of Mormon. What an
adventure we have when we read about the lives and toils of the

prophets. The first time I read the Book of Mormon I could hardly lay it down.

During one of my many readings of the Book of Mormon I decided to focus on just one thing—the style of writing—to see if I could see changes between the various writers or if it appeared that one man had written the entire book, as some suppose. The Lord enlightened my mind and I could almost tell you where one prophet concluded writing and another commenced. Although they are all prophets, they are as separate and distinct as the Twelve Apostles who walk the earth today.

Years later, on February 16, 1980, there was an article in the *Church News* titled, "Book of Mormon Has at Least 24 Writers." The article commenced, "Two statisticians who used computer techniques to analyze the Book of Mormon said they found 'overwhelming evidence' of multiple authorship of the book."

Evidence and testimony will ring down through future generations vindicating the prophets and the Church and witnessing to the world that the Book of Mormon is true.

Let me share with you some of the scriptures from the Book of Mormon that have touched my life in a meaningful way:

> But I, Nephi, have written what I have written, and I esteem it as of great worth, and especially unto my people. For I pray continually for them by day, and mine eyes water my pillow by night, because of them; and I cry unto my God in faith, and I know that he will hear my cry.
>
> And I know that the Lord God will consecrate my prayers for the gain of my people. And the words which I have written in weakness will be made strong unto them; for it persuadeth them to do good; it maketh known unto them of their fathers; and it speaketh of Jesus, and persuadeth them to believe in him, and to endure to the end, which is life eternal.
>
> And now, my beloved brethren, and also Jew, and all ye ends of the earth, hearken unto these words and believe in Christ; and if ye believe not in these words believe in Christ.
>
> And you that will not partake of the goodness of God, and respect the words of the Jews, and also my words, and the words which shall proceed forth out of the mouth of the Lamb of God, behold, I bid you an everlasting farewell, for these words shall condemn you at the last day.

For what I seal on earth, shall be brought against you at the
judgment far; for thus hath the Lord commanded me, and I must
obey. Amen. (2 Nephi 33:3–4, 10, 14–15.)

What a powerful witness! How could an honest-in-heart
person not feel the truth and witness of Nephi or not believe
these following words of King Benjamin:

And behold also, if I, whom ye call your king, who has spent his
days in your service, and yet has been in the service of God, do merit
any thanks from you, O how you ought to thank your heavenly
King!
I say unto you, my brethren, that if you should render all the
thanks and praise which your whole soul has power to possess, to
that God who has created you, and has kept and preserved you, and
has caused that ye should rejoice, and has granted that ye should live
in peace one with another—
I say unto you that if ye should serve him who has created you
from the beginning, and is preserving you from day to day, by
lending you breath, that ye may live and move and do according to
your own will, and even supporting you from one moment to
another—I say, if ye should serve him with all your whole souls yet
ye would be unprofitable servants.
And behold, all that he requires of you is to keep his commandments; and he has promised you that if ye would keep his commandments ye should prosper in the land; and he never doth vary from
that which he hath said; therefore, if ye do keep his commandments
he doth bless you and prosper you. (Mosiah 2:19–22.)

Also, he said to his people:

And also, ye yourselves will succor those that stand in need of
your succor; ye will administer of your substance unto him that
standeth in need; and ye will not suffer that the beggar putteth up his
petition to you in vain, and turn him out to perish.
Perhaps thou shalt say: The man has brought upon himself his
misery; therefore I will stay my hand, and will not give unto him of
my food, nor impart unto him of my substance that he may not
suffer, for his punishments are just—
But I say unto you, O man, whosoever doeth this the same hath
great cause to repent; and except he repenteth of that which he hath
done he perisheth forever, and hath no interest in the kingdom of
God.
For behold, are we not all beggars? Do we not all depend upon
the same Being, even God, for all the substance which we have, for

both food and raiment, and for gold, and for silver, and for all the riches which we have of every kind? (Mosiah 4:16–19.)

And in Alma we read Ammon's testimony before King Lamoni:

> And Ammon began to speak unto him with boldness, and said unto him: Believest thou that there is a God?
>
> And he answered, and said unto him: I do not know what that meaneth.
>
> And then Ammon said: Believest thou that there is a Great Spirit?
>
> And he said, Yea.
>
> And Ammon said: This is God. And Ammon said unto him again: Believest thou that this Great Spirit, who is God, created all things which are in heaven and in the earth?
>
> And he said: Yea, I believe that he created all things which are in the earth; but I do not know the heavens.
>
> And Ammon said unto him: The heavens is a place where God dwells and all his holy angels.
>
> And King Lamoni said: Is it above the earth?
>
> And Ammon said: Yea, and he looketh down upon all the children of men; and he knows all the thoughts and intents of the heart; for by his hand were they all created from the beginning.
>
> And king Lamoni said: I believe all these things which thou hast spoken. Art thou sent from God?
>
> Ammon said unto him: I am a man; and man in the beginning was created after the image of God, and I am called by his Holy Spirit to teach these things unto this people, that they may be brought to a knowledge of that which is just and true;
>
> And a portion of that Spirit dwelleth in me, which giveth me knowledge, and also power according to my faith and desires which are in God. (Alma 18:24–35.)

We can also read of the feelings of King Lamoni's father, who was king over all the Lamanites, after Aaron had taught him. The verses state:

> And it came to pass that after Aaron had expounded these things unto him, the king said: What shall I do that I may have this eternal life of which thou hast spoken? Yea, what shall I do that I may be born of God, having this wicked spirit rooted out of my breast, and receive his Spirit, that I may be filled with joy, that I may not be cast off at the last day? Behold, said he, I will give up all that I possess, yea, I will forsake my kingdom, that I may receive this great joy.
>
> But Aaron said unto him: If thou desirest this thing, if thou wilt bow down before God, yea, if thou wilt repent of all thy sins, and will

bow down before God, and call on his name in faith, believing that ye shall receive, then shalt thou receive the hope which thou desirest.

And it came to pass that when Aaron had said these words, the king did bow down before the Lord, upon his knees; yea, even he did prostrate himself upon the earth, and cried mightily, saying:

O God, Aaron hath told me that there is a God; and if there is a God, and if thou art God, wilt thou make thyself known unto me, and I will give away all my sins to know thee, and that I may be raised from the dead, and be saved at the last day. And now when the king had said these words, he was struck as if he were dead. (Alma 22:15–18.)

What a sweet, pure thought and prayer of one who feels the redeeming love of the Master!

Other favorite verses include:

O that cunning plan of the evil one! O the vainness, and the frailties, and the foolishness of men! When they are learned they think they are wise, and they hearken not unto the counsel of God, for they set it aside, supposing they know of themselves, wherefore, their wisdom is foolishness and it profiteth them not. And they shall perish.

But to be learned is good if they hearken unto the counsels of God. (2 Nephi 9:28–29.)

Also, in the same chapter, verse 41, we read:

O then, my beloved brethren, come unto the Lord, the Holy One. Remember that his paths are righteous. Behold, the way for man is narrow, but it lieth in a straight course before him, and the keeper of the gate is the Holy One of Israel; and he employeth no servant there; and there is none other way save it be by the gate; for he cannot be deceived, for the Lord God is his name.

Nephi, who was the son of Helaman, was a holy, chosen vessel in whom the Lord trusted:

And it came to pass that Nephi went his way towards his own house, pondering upon the things which the Lord had shown unto him.

And it came to pass as he was thus pondering—being much cast down because of the wickedness of the people of the Nephites, their secret works of darkness, and their murderings, and their plunderings, and all manner of iniquities—and it came to pass as he was thus pondering in his heart, behold, a voice came unto him saying:

Blessed art thou, Nephi, for those things which thou hast done; for I have beheld how thou hast with unwearyingness declared the word, which I have given unto thee, unto this people. And thou hast not feared them, and has not sought thine own life, but hast sought my will, and to keep my commandments.

And now, because thou hast done this with such unwearyingness, behold, I will bless thee forever; and I will make thee mighty in word and in deed, in faith and in works; yea, even that all things shall be done unto thee according to thy word, for thou shalt not ask that which is contrary to my will.

Behold, thou art Nephi, and I am God. Behold, I declare it unto thee in the presence of mine angels, that ye shall have power over this people, and shall smite the earth with famine, and with pestilence, and destruction, according to the wickedness of this people.

Behold, I give unto you power, that whatsoever ye shall seal on earth shall be sealed in heaven; and whatsoever ye shall loose on earth shall be loosed in heaven; and thus shall ye have power among this people.

And thus, if ye shall say unto this temple it shall be rent in twain, it shall be done.

And if ye shall say unto this mountain, Be thou cast down and become smooth, it shall be done.

And behold, if ye shall say that God shall smite this people, it shall come to pass.

And now behold, I command you, that ye shall go and declare unto this people, that thus saith the Lord God, who is the Almighty: Except ye repent ye shall be smitten, even unto destruction.

And behold, now it came to pass that when the Lord had spoken these words unto Nephi, he did stop and did not go unto his own house, but did return unto the multitudes who were scattered about upon the face of the land, and began to declare unto them the word of the Lord which had been spoken unto him, concerning their destruction if they did not repent. (Helaman 10:2–12.)

Note that after Nephi received this promise he "did not go into his own house, but did return unto the multitudes."

There are exciting chapters and books that are beyond the swellings of the heart and the emotions. They include all of 3 Nephi, the first few chapters of Ether, all of Moroni, and dozens and dozens more.

You will thrill as you read the scriptures personally and then use the computer to study them. You will embark on a study of the scriptures that will never come to an end but will lead you from one glorious plateau to another, ever onward and upward in your quest for understanding.

Balance and blend your study of the standard works with your own personal standard of works. The purpose for the wisdom and understanding of the life of Christ and all the words of the prophets is to assist us in our personal service to our fellow man. Francois de Chateaubriand said, "In days of service all things are founded; in days of special privilege they deteriorate; and in days of vanity they are destroyed."

Service to the Master should be the objective of all we know and learn. We but serve him as we serve and walk humbly and lowly among the shadow of the poor and sick, the orphan and widow, the despairing and heartsick, the weak and faithless. Nothing brings us closer to the Master than to walk in his steps.

In our youth we need the security of a repetitious study of the scriptures to keep us pure. There is so much that is evil around us. Never has there been such perversion, violence, pornography, permissiveness, compromise, lying, cheating, dishonesty, and disloyalty. Satan's influence is almost everywhere. Not only is he Satan but he is satanic. Not only is he evil but he is the devil. He laughs and mocks those of us who are in our second estate whom he binds down. He has no charity, not one particle. He has no purity, not a shred. He can never bring peace, only momentary pleasure and fleeting happiness. His mind is dark, there is no light, and he is an absolute and total enemy to God. Why should we listen to his tempting voice? How can we think that wickedness ever would be happiness. Think, my young friends. Arm yourselves with the powerful words of Christ. Read and study the scriptures daily until the habit becomes so strong it cannot be broken. The scriptures are a treasure beyond price.

There is security in the words of all the prophets. God bless you to love them, to read them, and to become what they teach us.

CHAPTER NINE

Bricks Without Straw

Moses and Aaron asked Pharaoh to free Israel. In the fifth chapter of Exodus, Pharaoh states: "Who is the Lord, that I should obey his voice to let Israel go? I know not the Lord, neither will I let Israel go." (Exodus 5:2.)

And instead of giving Israel her freedom, Pharaoh commanded the taskmasters of the people and their officers saying, "Ye shall no more give the people straw to make brick, as heretofore: let them go and gather straw for themselves" (Exodus 5:7). This was an additional great burden to the people, and Pharaoh did not reduce the quota for bricks he had previously laid on them.

The Israelites had to gather straw from the stubble in the field and continue to supply the specified quota. When they did not, they were beaten and cursed. Israel felt as if a great evil had come upon them. Moses, the great prophet, turned to God in prayer, and eventually Moses led the children of Israel from bondage.

We live in a generation where many of the youth attempt to build bricks without straw. In Moses' day straw was essential in making bricks that would not crumble, crack, or break. The straw was invaluable in providing a necessary inner adhesiveness.

In our day we live in an environment one stake president (and school professor) described as a manipulative society. Students attempt to manipulate teachers, professors, and others to improve a grade or to make an allowance or to reconsider a decision. This attitude seems to have sprung up in the last few years.

Many of you, our youth, have learned about investments or schemes that promise to produce a quick, fantastic return. Some of your families have lost lifetime savings, had to remortgage their homes, and start all over again financially. A common saying in my day was, "There ain't no such thing as a free lunch." My young friends, someone always pays.

When I was a boy and our home was being reroofed, I went up and sat by the roofer and talked to him while he worked. He was rough and he smoked, but he was pleasant with me and seemed not to mind my being up there with him. I suppose I might have provided a slight change from the monotony of roofing. During our conversation, he taught me a true principle, one that I will never forget. He said, "God helps those who help themselves."

Elbert Green Hubbard said it in a little different way:

The world bestows its big prizes, both in money and in honors, for but one thing.
And that is Initiative.
What is Initiative?
I'll tell you: It's doing the right thing without being told.
But next to doing the thing without being told is to do it when you are told once. That is to say, carry the Message to Garcia!
Next, there are those who never do a thing until they are told twice: such get no honors and small pay.
Next, there are those who do the right thing only when Necessity kicks them from behind, and these get indifference instead of honors, and a pittance for pay. This kind spends most of its time polishing a bench with a hard-luck story.
Then, still lower down in the scale than this, we find the fellow who will not do the right thing even when some one goes along to show him how, and stays to see that he does it: he is always out of a job, and receives the contempt he deserves, unless he has a rich Pa, in which case Destiny patiently awaits around the corner with a stuffed club.
To which class do you belong? ("Elbert Green Hubbard on Initiative," in *An American Bible,* ed. Alice Hubbard [East Aurora, New York: The Roycrofters, 1918], p. 305.)

In Moses' day bricks without straw simply lacked quality, and when heat and pressure and weight were applied, they crumbled and cracked.

In our society of youth in the Church, we must determine to be a genuine, quality product. Do not look for shortcuts in homework or physical conditioning. Be careful not to just get by at work. The Savior taught us to go the second mile, to return good for evil, to be perfect. No one can build a life of quality without the essential "straw."

Let me share with you some great concerns I have about conduct that is comparable to building bricks without straw.

There is great sin in the world and far too much sin in the Church. Some of our youth feel they can "eat, drink, and be merry" and delay keeping all the commandments until later when they are preparing for missions or temple marriage. In other words, some of our precious youth date before they are sixteen and a few get involved in petting and fornication. R-rated movies are seen in the home and the theater. Language that is abominable to the Lord is used. Pornography and dirty storytelling are seen and heard. Quite often a young person will seem totally active in the Church during these periods of sinning.

Oh, my young friends, there are dozens and dozens of ways we see our youth building disaster into the bricks of their lives.

A short while ago the phone rang and a priesthood leader spoke with me about a member of his ward who is twenty and is an alcoholic. He said: "I understand that your father was an alcoholic and you have an empathy for this problem. Can you give me some counsel that could be passed on to this young man so that he can prepare for a mission call? I believe he always wanted to go on a mission and probably planned to be called. He has wanted to go to the temple but now finds himself unworthy."

How would it feel to be an alcoholic at twenty, knowing that built into your character is the potentiality of cracking or crumbling every time the temptation to drink comes? If you asked this young man if he had planned on becoming an alcoholic, he would think you stupid to even ask, but someone must be stationed as a quality-control officer, as someone who will help him to accurately measure his life and determine his spiritual progress.

The General Authorities, stake presidents, bishops, and especially your parents, will ever be prepared to guide, direct, and assist you, but no one can make the decision for you.

Do not cheat on your college exams. Let integrity rule your life. Even in our own institutions I hear of tests being passed around among friends. Research and composition papers are submitted that are almost identical to those students had submitted a semester or two earlier. Other ingenious methods of cheating are used. Remember, though, no matter how ingenious the method seems, when the project is over it's still cheating.

Cheating creates an unfairness to the honest student in a class graded on the "curve." If every soul in the class were entirely honest, perhaps the "mean" average of all grades would be lower, but it would be accurate instead of artificially raising the curve with inflated test scores.

I remember as a boy that I had always felt a special sense of honesty. One young man who sat near me would cheat by copying my answers for those he did not know. He has grown up now and is a professional man. I have always wondered whether he still cheats.

At this very minute stop a moment and ponder; think of those you know who cheat. Several names will come to your mind. Now think about those you know who would never cheat no matter what the temptation or outcome might be.

Reread the dialogue from the movie *Camelot.* As you will recall from the movie, Mordred, King Arthur's illegitimate son, moves in to accelerate the ruin of the Round Table. Guinevere is to be burned at the stake. Lancelot makes a daring rescue and saves her. Finally, on a battlefield in France, just before dawn, Arthur is alone behind the lines. Lancelot brings Guinevere to King Arthur. Repair is impossible, the battle is inevitable, and Arthur's dream of Camelot is about over. He loves and forgives Guinevere and Lancelot. They leave, and he is once more left alone. Then he hears some rustling in the brush nearby, and we pick up the dialogue:

Arthur: Who's there? Who is out there? Come out, I say. [There then issues forth from the brush the blooming face of a boy.]

Tom:	Forgive me, your Majesty. I was searching for the Sergeant of Arms and got lost. I did not wish to disturb you.
Arthur:	Who are you? Where did you come from? Are you a page? You ought to be in bed.
Tom:	Forgive me, your Majesty, but I came to fight for the Round Table. I'm very good with a bow. I will kill the enemy.
Arthur:	But what if they kill you?
Tom:	Then I will be dead, m'Lord, but I don't intend to be killed. I intend to be a knight.
Arthur:	A knight?
Tom:	Yes, m'Lord, of the Round Table.
Arthur:	And when did you decide on this extinct profession? Was your welfare protected by knights? Was your father a knight? Was your mother saved by one?
Tom:	Oh, no, m'Lord. I had never seen a knight until I stowed away. I only know them by the stories people tell.
Arthur:	From the stories people tell you wish to become a knight? Now, tell me what you think you know of the knights of the Round Table?
Tom:	I know everything, m'Lord. Might for right, right for right, justice for all. A round table where all knights would sit. Everything.
Arthur:	Come here. What is your name?
Tom:	It is Tom of Warwick, Sir.
Arthur:	You will not fight. You will run behind the lines and live to return to England. You will do everything I, the king, tell you. [He sings] Each evening from December to December, before you drift to sleep upon your cot, think back on all the tales that you remember of Camelot. Ask everyone if he has heard the story, and tell it strong and loud and clear if he has not. . . . Camelot! Now, say it loud and with great joy. Camelot! Yes, come, my boy! . . . Don't let it be forgot, that once there was a spot, for one brief, shining moment that was known as Camelot!

Then, Pellinor, a friend of the king, enters the scene. He tells Arthur that it is time to prepare for battle.

Arthur:	Pellinor, give me your sword. [He then has young Tom come over and kneel before him.] With this sword, Excalibur, I knight thee Sir Tom of Warwick. I command you to return home and carry out my orders.
Tom:	Yes, m'Lord. [Young Tom runs off into the brush, his blond hair barely visible as he runs.]
Arthur:	Return home, run behind the lines, run, Tom!
Pellinor:	Who was that boy?
Arthur:	One of what we all are, Pelli. Less than a drop in the great blue ocean of the sunlit sea, but it seems that some of the drops sparkle. Some of them do sparkle, Pelli. Run, boy! Oh, run, my boy! (Alan Jay Lerner, *Camelot* [New York: Random House, 1961], p. 115.)

Some of the drops do sparkle. Those who use straw when they build bricks sparkle. There is no trait, or talent, or ability that can ever compensate for lack of character or integrity. If the "straw" is missing, enough applied pressure will bring about cracking, breaking, or eventual disintegration.

The Savior taught this same principle in the Sermon on the Mount:

> Therefore whosoever heareth these sayings of mine, and doeth them, I will liken him unto a wise man, which built his house upon a rock:
>
> And the rain descended, and the floods came, and the winds blew, and beat upon that house; and it fell not: for it was founded upon a rock.
>
> And every one that heareth these sayings of mine, and doeth them not, shall be likened unto a foolish man, which built his house upon the sand:
>
> And the rain descended, and the floods came, and the winds blew, and beat upon that house; and it fell; and great was the fall of it. (Matthew 7:24–27.)

Storms and rain will come, evil will descend, but faith in Christ and using straw in our bricks will build a solid character that can stand the greatest pressure and the most heat.

CHAPTER TEN

A Time of Sifting

Life forces on us myriad tests and challenges—some are subtle and insidious beyond belief, and quite often vanity is the great destroying motivator. I do not have the knowledge of anorexia nervosa or bulimia to discuss it professionally, yet there are theological principles that are constant and with which I am familiar. In this chapter, I will attempt to identify some moral disorders and teach principles as well as the consequences of such conduct or involvement.

You may wonder at the grouping of the following maladies. But, again remember that the concerns we face are real and very destructive. Consider the problems of our age: anorexia nervosa, bulimia, AIDS, homosexuality, lying, stealing, pornographic viewing, fads of dress and grooming (i.e., new wave and punk), hard-rock music, laziness, fornication, smoking, drinking, drugs, being on a dole, disrespect for parents, sexual abuses, gang beatings, cheating at school, manipulation of people, fantasizing, ostracizing persons from your group, rebellion, and so much more.

There are some constants that ought to be considered. The great God of heaven has instructed and taught us that obedience brings blessings and that wickedness never was and never will be happiness. Obedience is having enough maturity and wisdom to realize that as we live God's commandments we have true freedom. Satan's old lie is that God's rules and principles, his teachings and commandments, are restrictive and deprive us of our agency. Actually true freedom comes only through obedience to God's commandments. God's way will always be the best way, and those who have common sense realize that God, who loves us, would not want to bring down on us misery and unhappiness or evil and punishment.

On the other hand, Satan is the great deceiver, liar, and cheat. He has not one shred of integrity, wisdom, or light in his being. He seeks to make all men miserable like unto himself.

The violation of God's laws, in actuality, removes our free agency. Following corruption, evil and pleasure's paths bind us with a loss of agency stronger than chains, more confining than prison dungeons and more hopeless than a great abyss.

Consider with me the simplicity of the act of self-induced vomiting to keep from gaining weight. A person eats, or overeats, and is concerned about his or her weight and so induces vomiting. This is a form, as I understand it, of anorexia nervosa. Instead of gaining weight after a meal, actually there is weight loss. It is easier than practicing self-control and self-discipline, or moderation in eating. It works so well that it soon becomes an "acceptable" alternative to the true principle of self-discipline. It seems harmless enough in the beginning, but it quickly becomes a habit, a disease, a destroyer, and it ruins young lives. It is my understanding that there comes a point when no longer does the involved one need to induce vomiting. The physical body has been trained to regurgitate all that it takes in. The mind is no longer healthy; the physical body and its chemistry are out of balance. The involved one can no longer think or reason clearly and lacks the energy to resist this foolish, often fatal habit. There is such a distorted self-image that even when the person loses weight to the point of anemia or emaciation, she still sees herself as overweight. There are serious and profound psychological problems that become almost irreparable.

There will always be a consequence for sin or violation of God's commandments. We may choose to sin but we cannot eliminate the consequences. This is part of the eternal principle of justice. Chains of habit, loss of physical energy, and lack of reasoning ability slowly and carefully bind the involved one until he is a prisoner in the worst kind of hell. Another consequence is ruined health and, in some cases, even death. We know of some nationally prominent entertainers who have lost their health or even life from this dread disease.

The Lord's way to a trim, healthy body is in the Word of Wisdom. It requires sufficient sleep; good, hearty exercise; and a nutritionally balanced diet. There will never be an adequate substitute for personal discipline. All that life holds for us that is good comes from discipline. The root of the word *discipline* is *disciple*. Follow, as a disciple, the disciplines of the Master—then come attractiveness, vivaciousness, beauty, and the abundant and healthy life.

Homosexuality, fornication, petting, self-abuse, pornography, and all other sexual perversions bring about terrible consequences. Venereal diseases, along with AIDS debilitation and suffering, come from ignoring God's holy law of chastity. Purity in morality brings beauty, happiness, joy, freedom, strength, and power. One of the great powers God has given us is the power to procreate other human souls. A righteous and disciplined life will ensure confidence and virtue.

Satan whispers and entices us to "partake" and have the sensations of pleasure. There is no question in the minds of the prophets of either the past or the present that sin and sexual looseness bring momentary pleasure. If it did not, there would be no enticement. This again is how Satan uses the counterfeit of God's blessings and rewards to lead the children of men into darkness. The physical sensations are undeniable—it is part of God's plan—but when they are perverted, instead of blessings we suffer the consequences. Transgression damages, bruises, and wounds the spirit. It harms, infects, and diseases the physical body. By and by those who indulge for pleasure must suffer or repent. Many choose to repent only after they have suffered. (See D&C 19:4.)

Imagine what would happen to humanity if everyone lived a moral life—millions of babies would be born normal (without defects); divorce and family abandonment would be dramatically reduced; suffering and sickness for the most part would be lessened. There will always be physical problems to be endured even by good and honorable men and women. This is part of life and its testing, but much that we bring on ourselves could be eliminated.

Homosexuality is an abominable sin. How in all the world can any religious soul justify his or her actions on the basis of, "I was made this way"? That is the supreme cop-out. President Marion G. Romney once told me, "The Lord will not put a female spirit in a male body or a male spirit in a female body."

The homosexuals have only one God-given course open to them and that is absolute and total repentance. With that comes a washing and purging in the blood of the Lamb that brings forgiveness, and purity as white as snow. I am confident that God loves every son and daughter that walks the earth, but he deplores and finds despicable such acts of perversion. The Atonement cannot be wrought in the life of an individual except through repentance, faith in the Lord Jesus Christ, and keeping the commandments of the Lord. *There is no other way.*

Petting, self-abuse, and viewing pornography are serious because they lead to the major transgressions which bind and shackle the soul to the pleasures of the moment. Addiction to any sin is as real, whether mentally or physically, as those we commonly associate with drugs, drinking, or smoking.

A word ought to be said about some dress and grooming fads. Although they seem to be trivial in nature, they come from Lucifer. They do not represent individuality or uniqueness, but a satanic thrust based on rebellion and contempt. These are often not recognized in the beginning, but nonetheless they are there. This type of grooming brings compromise to standards and contention between youth and parents. The way to judge the seriousness of the act is to extend the consequences into the future and see what the act will bring. There are hundreds and thousands of ways to have appropriate grooming and dress standards.

The Lord's program is the best. No one would drink out of a polluted, stagnant stream of water when he could drink out of a cool, crystal-clear, pure fountain of water. The prophets have said, "Come to the shade of trees, come where cool breezes blow, where fresh flowers grow, where the sun is clear and the sky is fair—come and partake of living waters."

Satan is the author of frustration, contention, ridicule, rebellion, unhappiness, and misery. The way to judge whether grooming standards are appropriate is to use good people (your leaders, parents, and others with a sense of propriety and modesty) as models.

Another great concern of the Brethren is the amount of money our youth are spending for dates. Quite often this money is procured from a dad, or from wages that could go into a missionary fund. We want you to have a good time, but sometimes an expensive date is a substitute for substance of character or lack of social relation skills. True character can never be buried. As you know, personality is what others think of us; character and integrity are what we really are.

My young friends, you are no longer on a dole. A dole is money or unearned goods received. An example is this great nation. There are so many people on a welfare dole that those who work can hardly carry the financial burdens for those who will not or who are content to sit back and let someone else carry their load. Not only is this not Christian but it also will not work. A parallel example would be for a football player to sit back during practice and scrimmage and then expect that someone else can get in condition for him. It just will never happen. His friend could do twice as many physical exercises but he only becomes that much stronger. It will not do anything for his friend —except set a good example.

So it is with a dole, either for dating or for living; the one carrying the load can only carry so much before he will break.

Our beloved prophet, President Ezra Taft Benson, said: "The Lord works from the inside out. The world works from the outside in. The world would take people out of the slums. Christ takes the slums out of people, and then they take themselves out of the slums. The world would mold men by changing their environment. Christ changes men, who then change their environment. The world would shape human behavior, but Christ can change human nature." (Conference Report, October 1985, p. 5.) Be aware, my young friends, that dating can be wonderful but it does not have to be expensive to be good. In fact, being with a good person or the right person is everything. There are pitifully sad women who have married for money. They have almost everything that money can buy but have wretched lives. There are those who are poor, who struggle desperately, and their marriages are exquisite. There are others who are married to the right person who happens to have money and they are happy too. Self-esteem and self-respect come as we are independent, thrifty, and use our precious means to further the Lord's work.

Cheating may be the lowest level to which a student can sink. Of course there are graver sins, but for the student cheating is a lying, deceitful, and scholastic dole that is evil. When a young person graduates from high school or college, his gradepoint means only as much as the integrity behind it. Someone who uses someone else's thesis, steals test questions or answers, or copies someone else's paper is the hollow shell of a graduate. There is no substance behind the facade. Honest men and women in business are far more impressed with a man or woman whose true character is behind his or her gradepoint.

We discussed the law of compensation earlier in this chapter. There will always be compensating blessings for the truthful, honest student of integrity, as there will always be eventual consequences for the cheater. Those who cheat have developed a terrible, destructive habit. They may cheat on a husband or wife later, or on an employer or customer. They cannot be trusted, and that is the gravest consequence. It is better to be trusted than loved and far better if we can be loved and trusted.

Young people in their supposed innocence sometimes can be cruel beyond belief. To exclude peer members and to form cliques or ties to someone or some group and exclude others is not Christian. The gospel of Jesus Christ is inclusive. It reaches out and encircles all the ugly or homely, the handicapped or impaired, the rich or poor, the bright or dull; none are excluded except through their own choice or transgression. Even the repentant transgressor is included. Should we do less than the Master has taught us? My young friends, the mature individual includes all, the insecure person excludes others as a way of building his or her own image. But everyone can see through it. It is fake and empty and unkind.

Work is a strong Christian ethic. Laziness and idleness are evil. The same principles that apply to other vices apply here. Learn to work. Learn it at home. Clean your room and keep it clean, assist with the dishes, vacuum the floor, do the yard work, weed the flower beds, paint the fences, feed the animals. All of the chores you do are work. They give you discipline and they teach you skills that will be used in your job and the rest of your life. Work is an eternal blessing with generous benefits of clear thinking, mental well-being, physical health, confidence, and a sense of self-reliance.

We have only "broad brushed" a few subjects that need to be treated here. Someone said, "Though argument does not change belief, the lack of it destroys belief." If you have a flaw in your character on any of the things mentioned in this chapter, go to your parents humbly and ask for help. If you cannot for some reason go to your parents, go to your bishop. He will always be available when you are in trouble. He has the mantle of authority in your ward as the presiding high priest and he is entitled to revelation in your behalf. There is a power in the priesthood. Seek a blessing if you need one for strength. Go first to your father or another priesthood-holding relative. If they are not available, then call on your home teachers or a quorum leader. There may be some rare cases where you will seek a blessing from the bishop.

In conclusion, remember that there are principles of truth to guide you. Consider these:

—Wickedness never was happiness.

—Habits bind us to a course of action previously determined.

—The consequences of sin are misery, sadness, sickness, unhappiness, and suffering.

—The Lord said that we must repent or suffer.

—Charity (the pure love of Christ) never fails.

—"Work will win when wishy-washy wishing won't." (President Thomas S. Monson)

—Life is a test.

—Every true principle and doctrine has a counterfeit by the master of lies.

—Avoid any act or conduct which causes contention, removes the Lord's Spirit, causes suffering on the part of someone else, or will bring misery and regret.

—Ask yourself the question, "How would the best people, the people I respect most, feel about this?"

—Ask yourself, "Is this the real thing or Satan's counterfeit?" Compare it with the teachings of the Master.

This is a time of sifting, of separating righteous people from unrighteous ones. Joshua said, "Choose you this day whom ye will serve; whether the gods which your fathers served that were on the other side of the flood, or the gods of the Amorites [false gods], in whose land ye dwell: but as for me and my house, we will serve the Lord" (Joshua 24:15).

Choose wisely and with maturity; your eternal welfare is the consequence.

Magnificent Promises

Every soul will sometime during his life be tempted or invited to drink some alcoholic beverage. The Word of Wisdom is one of the most exciting and beautiful of all the Master's teachings. Imagine the value of good health—to run and not be weary, to walk and not faint. (See D&C 89:20.)

We often think of the Word of Wisdom as a restriction of our agency. It is not. It does not take away our freedom but rather ensures it. My father smoked two to three packages of cigarettes a day. He was not free. Even at night he would be awakened by the physical need to smoke every two or three hours. When he received a paycheck, he was not free. The chains of alcoholism dragged him to any location at which he could indulge in a drink. That would continue for two or three days until the money was gone. No one could call that being free. I have heard my dad say, "I have prayed to God to take my life rather than to do this to my family." The prayer was as empty as his commitment to quit.

What a marvelous revelation we have in the Word of Wisdom! We are taught to abstain. Drugs, smoking, drinking, coffee, tea, and pornography are all addictive.

Samuel Smiles states:

The young man, as he passes through life, advances through a long line of temptors ranged on either side of him; and the inevitable effect of yielding is degradation in a greater or a lesser degree. Contact with them tends insensibly to draw away from him some portion of the divine electric element with which his nature is charged; and his only mode of resisting them is to utter and act out his "No" manfully and resolutely. He must decide at once, not waiting to deliberate and balance reasons: for the youth, like "the woman who deliberates, is lost." Temptation will come to try the young man's strength; and, once yielded to, the power to resist grows weaker and weaker. Yield once, and a portion of virtue is gone. Resist manfully, and the first decision will give strength for life; repeated, it will become a habit. It is in the outworks of the habits formed in early life that the real strength of the defense must lie; for it has been wisely ordained that the machinery of moral existence should be carried on principally through the medium of the habits, so as to save the wear and tear of the great principles within. It is good habits, which insinuate themselves into the thousand inconsiderable acts of life, that really constitute by far the greater part of man's moral conduct.

Hugh Miller has told how, by an act of youthful decision, he saved himself from one of the strong temptations so peculiar to a life of toil. When employed as a mason, it was usual for his fellow-workmen to have an occasional treat of drink, and one day two glasses of whisky fell to his share, which he swallowed. When he reached home he found, on opening his favorite book—"Bacon's Essays"—that the letters danced before his eyes, and that he could no longer master the sense. "The condition," he says, "into which I had brought myself was, I felt, one of degradation. I had sunk, by my own act, for the time, to a lower level of intelligence than that on which it was my privilege to be placed; and, though the state could have been no very favorable one for forming a resolution, I in that hour determined that I should never again sacrifice my capacity of intellectual enjoyment to a drinking usage; and, with God's help, I was enabled to hold by the determination." It is such decisions as this that often form the turning points in a man's life, and furnish the foundation of his future character. And this rock, on which Hugh Miller might have been wrecked, if he had not at the right moment put forth his moral strength to strike away from it, is one that youth and manhood alike need to be constantly on their guard against. It is about one of the worst and most deadly, as well as extravagant, temptations which lie in the way of youth. Sir Walter Scott used to say that, "of all vices, drinking is the most incompatible with greatness." Not only so, but it is incompatible with economy, decency, health and honest living. Dr. Johnson said, referring to his own habits, "Sir, I can abstain; but I can't be moderate." (Samuel

Smiles, *Happy Homes and the Hearts that Make Them* [Chicago: U.S. Publishing House, 1882], pp. 388–90.)

Think about the wisdom in the preceding paragraphs, the wisdom that has been available to the teachable for centuries. Samuel Smiles's book, published 104 years ago, is filled with principles and philosophies that do not change. Substance abuse will have the same effect on the human anatomy 200 years from now as it does today. Principles remain constant.

I read an article on a great running back. In the first game, he did some serious damage to his knee on the first play he ran. It required surgery. Everyone wondered how long it would be before he would return. He wisely said: "I am finished. I do not want to do any more damage to my knee. I have an entire life ahead of me."

This same principle is true about substance-abuse considerations. Why take a chance of involvement when you have the rest of your life to live?

Visit a nursery at a hospital sometime and see the newborn babies. It is heartbreaking to see babies whose parents were on drugs at the time of conception and during pregnancy. Some are born with malformations, blindness, or other serious handicaps. By contrast, the Word of Wisdom gives us exciting promises which endure throughout our lives and reach into the lives of our children and grandchildren.

Quite often when a person does not live the Word of Wisdom, it is because he has a rebellious spirit. As a young man (twelve or thirteen) I used to mow lawns with my younger brother. We walked almost three miles to the homes where we mowed the lawns. It was during the summer and we mowed them in the heat of the day. We used a push mower, and we edged the lawn and flagstones with hand clippers. One particularly hot day, after we had been working for a couple of hours, the kind woman whose lawn we mowed apparently felt sorry for us. The hot sun seemed to boil down on us. We were both perspiring and almost, it seemed, to the point of heat exhaustion. She came out of the house carrying a little tray of ice-cold cola drinks in bottles. I remember to this day the temptation. Cold beads of water were dripping down the bottles and we felt we were in need.

The previous week a quorum leader, our Scoutmaster, had taught us that certain drinks contained caffeine. At that time I decided I would never drink any beverage which contained caffeine.

Without a moment of hesitation, I said to this kind woman, "Thank you, but we do not drink caffeine drinks." A few moments later we were getting a drink of water out of the garden hose. It seems I have always had a believing heart and, like Elder Sterling W. Sill, I have had an appetite for spiritual things.

All of us remember the oft-repeated story about the young mother who was leaving the house for a few minutes and said to her three-year-old son: "Now, son, do not climb up on the counter and get into the canister of beans. And whatever you do, do not stuff one up your nose." Of course, the little guy did exactly what his mom told him not to do.

Sometimes we forget that there are many refreshing beverages that do not contain drugs—various flavored soft drinks, fruit juices, and others. There are so many good choices that we need not drink something just because we are told we shouldn't.

Some years back I knew of a sweet widow whose son had become an alcoholic. He married and then abandoned his wife. When he was sober he was an excellent worker, so he usually had a job. Over the years conditions deteriorated to the point that he had no work and lived off of unemployment or welfare benefits. During the last several years of his mother's life, he made no contact with her. She had no idea as to his whereabouts. I know that she prayed faithfully every morning and night for her wayward son. It reminds me of the poem—

Where Is My Wandering Boy Tonight?

Where is my wandering boy tonight? the boy of my tend'rest care:
The boy that was once my joy and light, the child of my love and prayer.

Chorus:
    Oh, where is my boy tonight? where is my boy tonight?
    My heart o'erflows, for I love him, he knows,
    Oh, where is my boy tonight?

Once he was pure as the morning dew, as he knelt at his mother's
    knee;
No face was so bright, no heart more true, and none was as sweet
    as he. (*Chorus.*)
Oh, could I see him now, my boy, as fair as in olden time,
When prattle and smile made home a joy, and life was a merry
    chime. (*Chorus.*)
Go, for my wandering boy tonight, go search for him where you
    will:
But bring him to me with all his blight, and tell him I love him
    still. (*Chorus.*) (Ralph L. Woods, ed., *A Treasury of the Familiar*
    [Macmillan Publishing Co., Inc., 1978], p. 465.)

Undoubtedly this was the prayer of my widow friend. She did
not know where her wandering boy was.

This wonderful woman had a stroke and was admitted into the
hospital. She hung precariously between life and death and then
seemed to respond to care and treatment. Later she was transferred to a rest home where my wife and I visited her. During the
last days before her death, there seemed to be a haunting look in
her eyes. It was a type of despair and loneliness, I think for her
son.

A few weeks later she passed away, and I was invited to speak
at the funeral service. On the day of the funeral I was up early.
During the night and early morning hours when I was half asleep,
I had a thought that kept trailing through my mind. I felt that I
was to find this widow's son and get him to the funeral. I took an
extra suit from my closet, a pair of shoes, stockings, a white shirt,
and a tie. I told my wife I would meet her at the mortuary.

A phone call was made to the son's former wife, but she said
that she had promised her separated husband that she would
never divulge his address to the family. I drove to her home and
pleaded with her. She maintained her position. Then a lady who
was visiting her said, "You tell me and I will tell Elder Featherstone." This man's abandoned wife gave his address to her friend
and her friend gave it to me. I could not find the street in the
phone book. I drove to the part of town where I suspected he

lived. I drove up and down the streets searching, looking, without any success. I drove for over an hour. Then a policeman came along and I asked him if he knew where the street was located. He did.

I drove to the street and could not find the exact address—there wasn't any. Then, a thought struck me that there might be an apartment in the back. There was no apartment, only a garage. I walked back to the garage and saw a door on the side. I could hear a television going inside. I knocked and no one answered. I pushed the door open and there was a woman who was probably forty but looked about eighty. She was dirty and unkempt. She sat on a couch that was broken down—little fabric, springs sticking through—and she was drinking beer.

I said to her: "Please, I am looking for [this man]. Can you help me find him?" She was very rude and said: "No, get out of my house. I will not tell you where he is." "Is this where he lives?" "Yes, but where he is, is none of your business." I said: "It is my business. It's very important." While I was talking, I looked around the room and could even see into the bedroom.

Hardly a soul who reads this book could picture the filth and clutter—the stacks of dirty dishes, newspapers, magazines, dirty clothes, and a stench beyond anything imaginable. He was not home. I could see that.

I said to her: "I do not want to be offensive but his mother died. The funeral is today and I have come to take him to it." An interesting thing happened. This woman softened, her countenance changed, and tears welled up in her eyes. She said, "I don't know where he is, but he went to a place where they provide temporary employment." I thanked her and left, searching for a phone booth to get an address. I located the company and inquired if they had placed him. They had.

I went to the plant where he was working and found the foreman. I asked him if this man was working there temporarily. He said that he was. I said: "His mother died and the funeral is today. He does not know about it and I doubt that he has clothes to wear to attend it. If you will let him off, I will pay his wage for the rest of the day and get him back here after the services." This fine man said: "Elder Featherstone, I recognize you. See if he will go with you. If he will, we will pay him for the full day. You will not need to pay him." He pointed to this man. He was a good-sized man, probably six foot two and 230 pounds. I had made up my mind that if he resisted I would drag him there if necessary. I approached him, said hello, told him my errand, and then before he could respond I said: "I have a suit, shirt, tie, and shoes in the car. We can go to your mother's apartment to change." I was all ready to exert whatever force necessary when he said, "I will go with you if I can get off." "That is all arranged, come with me," I replied, and we hurried out to the car. We drove to the apartment, where he showered and changed and then we went to the funeral.

One of the most touching experiences of my life happened when I drove into the mortuary. His sister, who had not seen him for years (a wonderful Latter-day Saint woman, full of faith), was waiting outside in front of the mortuary. It was just fifteen minutes before the funeral. She saw me drive in with her brother and she burst into tears. I dropped him off and went to park. I saw in the rearview mirror this good woman run to him and embrace him. It was a great, emotional moment.

Later on during the service my eyes rested on this "wandering boy" of fifty who was back with his mother one last time. I remember the deep feelings that his mother would be pleased. I wept silently while awaiting my turn to speak.

I imagine somewhere in God's heaven a sweet widow continues to pray "Where is my wandering boy tonight?" And I also think of him and wonder: "What are the consequences of not living the commandments. I know he isn't happy, nor ever could be, living under such conditions."

The Word of Wisdom has such magnificent promises when obeyed and such severe consequences when ignored or violated. Do not be a slave to habits that overpower your agency. Be free, truly free. Walk in the light of the Lord and you will know such freedom as you never imagined. Trust in the Lord. He will never fail you and will ever be there to help when you are really in trouble.

I thank God with all my heart for the Word of Wisdom.

Forgiveness Is Available

Many of our youth have made serious mistakes, some of major consequence. When this happens, the Spirit withdraws and self-esteem suffers. Quite often frustration, depression, sadness, and emptiness accompany the one who has sinned. An attitude of "what's the use trying, I have sinned beyond repair" takes over. Satan is always there to capitalize on our moments of weakness. He whispers ever so subtly, "You are lost; you cannot repent; a mission and temple marriage are out of the question." Then, in the way of his wickedness, he counsels: "God will not hear your prayers. There is no use in going to church because you will be asked to participate in the sacrament and you are not worthy. Get involved with those who do wickedness also; they will accept you and be your friends no matter what you do. Those who attend church are self-righteous. Don't listen to them. They would never understand. Don't pay attention to your parents. They just get angry and never listen. Come, come, come with me. Eat, drink, and be merry; repent later, but for now come and partake of the pleasures of life. The sensations and pleasures will come; the banquet is spread before you, partake without restraint."

Oh, the evil liar, who is filled with deception and who binds us with the chains of transgression and drags us carefully down to hell to become miserable like unto himself. (See 2 Nephi 28:21.) He is the enemy. There is no truth in him, no mercy, no justice, only hate, envy, lies, and deceit. What a tragedy when those who transgress tune out the whisperings, counsel, and eventual peace that awaits those who humbly repent and turn to him who bringeth peace.

Recently I met with a young woman who was in her late teens. She had been involved with a young man not of our faith. She had not planned to marry him but rather was involved for the pleasure of the moment. She became pregnant. The evil one whispered to her to get an abortion. In a thousand ways, constantly, incessantly, he attempted to persuade her to get an abortion. He tried to keep her from counseling with her bishop. He whispered into her mind lies about her parents. He tried to deceive her about the bishop. He tried to persuade her to abandon her friends who were active in the Church.

Thank goodness she did not listen. Her bishop and parents counseled and prayed with her. They arranged to have her leave her home and stay in a distant state with a wonderful family in Salt Lake City. She received constant reinforcement and she attended church. No one except the family knew of her transgression. She helped the foster family by babysitting, cleaning the house, doing yard work, and assisting in every way she could.

Instead of an abortion she had a beautiful, dark-eyed, dark-haired, fair-complected baby. The act itself of giving birth caused a purging to take place in her life. She became the means of bringing a beautiful baby to a wonderful, deserving couple who had biologically been denied this privilege. The couple shed tears of emotion as they took this little soul into their arms.

I had the privilege of giving the unwed mother a blessing, and under the Lord's inspiration I told her that the determination not to submit to an abortion but to have the baby and provide a child to a deserving couple was the means of bringing partial forgiveness for the major transgression committed. Charity (the pure love of Christ) covers a multitude of sins. Although she had been involved in serious immoral problems, she exercised charity and repentance. She was and will be blessed.

It would seem that this is the wisest and best course in such circumstances. There are many reasons for this. Often the girl's mother must work outside the home, and in any case, rearing the child is not her direct responsibility. There would be the expense of hiring a baby-sitter from whatever income the young mother could earn. She would have to explain the baby to young men she dated. These are some reasons why in most cases it is right to hand the young soul over to a fine family in which the child can be lovingly cared for and reared in the Church by a faithful mother and father.

This chapter deals with those who have been involved in transgression, many of whom have lost hope that they can repent. Victor Hugo states in *Les Miserables* that "the shepherd does not recoil from the diseased sheep."

During the period of transgression, the Lord provides people who care and who can help the transgressor. What a tragedy for the sinful one to feel that a total descent, a complete abandonment of faith, must take place before he desires to repent. We do not have to drink the full cup of iniquity to realize the bitter taste. The sooner repentance takes place, the easier it is. The longer we transgress, the less ability we have to repent.

Consider this incident as recorded in *Les Miserables:*

> He felt that he was entering the water, and that he had under his feet, pavement no longer, but mud.
>
> It sometimes happens, on certain coasts of Brittany or Scotland, that a man, traveller or fisherman, walking on the beach at low tide far from the bank, suddenly notices that for several minutes he has been walking with some difficulty. The strand beneath his feet is like pitch; his soles stick to it; it is sand no longer, it is glue. The beach is perfectly dry, but at every step he takes, as soon as he lifts his foot, the print which it leaves fills with water. The eye, however, has noticed no change; the immense strand is smooth and tranquil, all the sand has the same appearance, nothing distinguishes the surface which is solid from the surface which is no longer so; the joyous little cloud of sand-fleas continues to leap tumultuously over the wayfarer's feet. The man pursues his way, goes forward, inclines towards the land, endeavours to get nearer the upland. He is not anxious. Anxious about what? Only, he feels somehow as if the

weight of his feet increased with every step which he takes. Suddenly he sinks in. He sinks in two or three inches. Decidedly he is not on the right road; he stops to take his bearings. All at once, he looks at his feet. His feet have disappeared. The sand covers them. He draws his feet out of the sand, he will retrace his steps, he turns back, he sinks in deeper. The sand comes up to his ankles, he pulls himself out and throws himself to the right, the sand comes up to his shins. Then he recognizes with unspeakable terror that he is caught in the quicksand, and that he has beneath him the fearful medium in which man can no more walk than the fish can swim. He throws off his load if he has one, he lightens himself like a ship in distress; it is already too late, the sand is above his knees.

He calls, he waves his hat or his handkerchief, the sand gains on him more and more; if the beach is deserted, if the land is too far off, if the sandbank is of too ill-repute, if there is no hero in sight, it is all over, he is condemned to enlizement. He is condemned to that appalling interment, long, infallible, implacable, impossible to slacken or to hasten, which endures for hours, which will not end, which seizes you erect, free and in full health, which draws you by the feet, which, at every effort that you attempt, at every shout that you utter, drags you a little deeper, which appears to punish you for your resistance by a redoubling of its grasp, which sinks the man slowly into the earth while it leaves him all the time to look at the horizon, the trees, the green fields, the smoke of the villages in the plain, the sails of the ships upon the sea, the birds flying and singing, the sunshine, the sky. Enlizement is the grave become a tide and rising from the depths of the earth towards a living man. Each minute is an inexorable enshroudress. The victim attempts to sit down, to lie down, to creep; every movement he makes, inters him; he straightens up, he sinks in; he feels that he is being swallowed up; he howls, implores, cries to the clouds, wrings his hands, despairs. Behold him waist deep in the sand; the sand reaches his breast, he is now only a bust. He raises his arms, utters furious groans, clutches the beach with his nails, would hold by that straw, leans upon his elbows to pull himself out of this soft sheath, sobs frenziedly; the sand rises. The sand reaches his shoulders, the sand reaches his neck; the face alone is visible now. The mouth cries, the sand fills it; silence. The eyes still gaze, the sand shuts them; night. Then the forehead decreases, a little hair flutters above the sand; a hand protrudes, comes through the surface of the beach, moves and shakes, and disappears. Sinister effacement of a man. (Victor Hugo, *Les Miserables*, trans. Charles E. Wilbur [Random House, 1862], pp. 1083–84.)

It is easy to draw a parallel to sin. Someone stated that there is a time when people could repent if they would. Then, if they do not repent, the time comes later when they would repent if they could. I have a firm belief in God's love for his children. I have an absolute testimony about the atoning sacrifice of the Lord Jesus. The Lord said to Isaiah, "Though your sins be as scarlet, they shall be as white as snow; though they be red like crimson, they shall be as wool" (Isaiah 1:18). Also, the Lord states in the Doctrine and Covenants: "Nevertheless, ye are blessed, for the testimony which ye have borne is recorded in heaven for the angels to look upon; and they rejoice over you, and your sins are forgiven you" (D&C 62:3).

James, chapter 5, verse 20, states, "Let him know, that he which converteth the sinner from the error of his way shall save a soul from death, and shall hide a multitude of sins."

Forgiveness can come but it will not be easy. If all people understood the Atonement and the opportunities afforded the repentant, they would crawl across cut glass to the outstretched arms of the Shepherd if necessary. But it is not necessary. "His way is easy."

Some time ago Elder Hugh Pinnock shared a poem with me that I have committed to memory.

> They do me wrong who say I come no more
> When once I knock and fail to find you in,
> For every day I stand outside your door
> And bid you wake, and rise to fight and win.
>
> Wail not for precious chances passed away,
> Weep not for golden ages on the wane!
> Each night I burn the records of the day;
> At sunrise every soul is born again.
> (Walter Malone, "Opportunity," in
> *A Treasury of Inspiration,* ed. Ralph L. Woods
> [New York: Thomas Y. Crowell Company,
> 1951], p. 83.)

I would fight and bleed and die to preserve the truths stated in the last two lines. To our youth who have been involved in any kind of sin, we plead along with the prophets: "Come, come, to the shade of trees, to the clear cooling waters, come to green pastures, come and bathe in living waters. Wash the dirt and soil from your soul, extinguish the burning flames that consume your mind, walk in the sun and in the moon. Come, remove the burden and be cleansed." The Lord said, "I the Lord remember [your sins] no more" (D&C 58:42). Trust him, believe him, lay aside your evil past and come, please come, and partake.

Over the years I have been able to observe our beloved youth who have violated the teachings and commandments of God. They may have pleasure for a moment, they may find excitement that produces a sensation of happiness, they may find friends and a distorted sense of self-worth as they belong to a group whose conduct is similar; however, it has been my experience that they never truly find joy or happiness but only their counterfeit. "Men are, that they might have joy" (2 Nephi 2:25).

The Lord wants us to be happy, and no amount of wickedness will ever bring happiness. Even when our sins go undiscovered or if they be in the darkness, there is no place in all of eternity that a sinner can remove his sins except in "the blood of the Lamb." There is no other name given under heaven, no other good enough to pay the price for our sins. Only he could "unlock the door" through which we may enter.

The Lord will never let Satan tempt you more than you can withstand. Paul teaches us that "there hath no temptation taken you but such as is common to man: but God is faithful, who will not suffer you to be tempted above that ye are able; but will with the temptation also make a way to escape, that ye may be able to bear it" (1 Corinthians 10:13).

As stated earlier, the Lord reaches out to us through our parents, other family members, home teachers, advisers, bishops, and righteous friends.

Now is the time to repent. Work up the courage and talk to your parents and bishop. We need you back in the fold. You need what the gospel of repentance can do for you. Gospel means the Lord's good message. The gospel of repentance means the Lord's good message about repentance—that it is possible. We can have our sins removed.

Remember the Church and its leaders will not remove themselves from you. Forgiveness is available. You must take the responsibility yourself if you are not active or involved in sin. The doors are open wide to every repentant sinner. If you have removed yourself, return again. The peace that has been lacking in your life can return.

Poverty: The Mother
of Miseries

It has been said that poverty is the "mother of miseries." In *Roget's Thesaurus* there is a multitude of synonyms and phrases that help one to understand the bondage of debt. Let me list just a few: embarrassed, indigence, penury, pauperism, beggarliness, privation, hand-to-mouth existence, the poor and needy, poor man, down-and-outer, destitute, bankrupt, and many others.

No one can know beforehand the calamity and the sadness brought about by debt. The purpose of this chapter is to remind *all,* young and old, of the Christian responsibilities of dealing with debt. Debt is an obligation. It is a man's bond. Any good Latter-day Saint will do everything in his power to take care of indebtedness.

We have been counseled to avoid debt like a plague. Debt puts us in bondage. Those in bondage cannot think as clearly or reason as rationally as those free of debt.

We have an unusual perversion of honesty taking place in the lives of far too many Latter-day Saints. It is more serious in the Church than we would ever believe. One source states that 89 percent of all divorces are somehow involved in financial problems at home; that is, the problem was either created or added to because of financial problems in the home. Consider the following cases; all of them are true, only names and locations have been deleted:

One recently married young man said that on his wedding day, after they had been sealed in the temple, his bride discussed with him the fact that she owed twelve thousand dollars in charges on credit cards. Her mother was related to a very wealthy family, and because she did not have sufficient money to keep up with the rest of the family, she had abused the charge card privileges. Her daughter had learned to follow this example. Thus, a young man (a fine Latter-day Saint from a good LDS home, going to school, working part-time) married a girl and found that immediately he had a twelve-thousand-dollar debt hanging over his head. Her parents could not handle the debt, or they would not; thus, this marriage was rocky from the very beginning.

One man has simply abandoned all principles regarding honesty and integrity. He buys videotape recorders and uses them for three or four months, knowing that they will be repossessed. He has done this with several cars for himself and for his family—nice cars. He has done it with furniture, with a boat, and with snowmobiles. He recently bought his son a new convertible and let him drive it for several months before the finance company finally repossessed it. This man carries a current, active temple recommend and supposedly is in good standing in the Church.

A young man had his father sign a major note with him. The son made no attempt to pay the note. The bank took the son's name off the note and left the father with a major loan to pay off. When the father discussed these matters with his son and his son's wife, the wife said, "Well, there are things more important than money and we are focusing on those things." She did not talk about this tremendous debt of thousands of dollars that they had dumped onto their father.

We find good Latter-day Saints taking out bankruptcy with no thought of ever paying back the monies. One member of a high council took out bankruptcy and immediately moved into a home valued at approximately $180,000 with a large swimming pool. He drives a brand new car while all his creditors are left holding the bag.

Another family moved into a home built by a member of a bishopric who is in the construction business. Because he was LDS, the member of the bishopric bent over backwards to get the man and his family into the home. He lived there for about a year without making one payment on the mortgage. Finally he was removed from the home, but by this time this fine, honorable, LDS contractor was held with all the back payments on the mortgage, putting his own family in a serious condition. The man who moved out moved into another ward. He is not active in the Church, receives welfare, and has no desire (makes no commitment) to pay these things off.

We have families living in homes with mortgages of six or eight hundred or even one thousand dollars a month who desire to have the mortgages paid by their bishops. Our youth seem to borrow monies from the government for education with no intention to ever pay back the money to the government. We have other members using their friends to help get credit by lying and giving inaccurate information.

God will hold us accountable for this type of conduct. We must be an honest people. Thank God the majority of Latter-day Saints are honest. We have the reputation of being a fair, honest people of integrity. In Georgia a nonmember family runs a cleaning establishment. They sell men's suits at reduced rates out of the back room. They have no advertising and no selling costs. One of our priesthood leaders went to this business, bought two suits, and then discovered he did not have his wallet. The lady said, "You are LDS, aren't you?" He replied that he was. She said: "You take the suits and mail me a check or bring the money in later. I know you are honest."

Can you imagine the damage that would have been done if this man had violated that great trust, or if anyone does in the future?

Samuel Smiles wrote in 1882:

> The proverb says that "an empty bag can not stand upright;" neither can a man who is in debt. It is also difficult for a man who is in debt to be truthful; hence it is said that lying rides on debt's back.

The debtor has to frame excuses to his creditor for postponing payment of the money he owes him, and probably also to contrive falsehoods. It is easy enough for a man who will exercise a healthy resolution, to avoid incurring the first obligation; but the facility with
which that has been incurred often becomes a temptation to a
second; and very soon the unfortunate borrower becomes so en-
tangled that no late exertion of industry can set him free. The first
step in debt is like the first step in falsehoods; almost involving the
necessity of proceeding in the same course, debt following debt, as
lie follows lie. Haydon, the painter, dated his decline from the day
on which he first borrowed money. He realized the truth of the
proverb, "Who goes a-borrowing, goes a-sorrowing." The signifi-
cant entry in his diary is, "Here began debt and obligation, out of
which I have never been and never shall be extricated as long as I
live." His autobiography shows but too painfully how embarrassment in money matters produces poignant distress of mind, utter
incapacity for work, and constantly recurring humiliations. The
written advice which he gave to a youth when entering the navy was
as follows: "Never purchase any enjoyment if it can not be procured
without borrowing of others. Never borrow money; it is degrading. I
do not say never lend, but never lend if by lending you render
yourself unable to pay what you owe; but under any circumstances
never borrow." Fichte, the poor student, refused to accept even
presents from his still poorer parents.

Dr. [Samuel] Johnson held that early debt is ruin. His words on
the subject are weighty, and worthy of being held in remembrance.
"Do not," said he, "accustom yourself to consider debt only as an
inconvenience; you will find it a calamity. Poverty takes away so
many means of doing good, and produces so much inability to resist
evil, both natural and moral, that it is by all virtuous means to be
avoided. . . . Let it be your first care, then, not to be in any man's
debt. Resolve not to be poor; whatever you have, spend less. Poverty
is a great enemy to human happiness; it certainly destroys liberty,
and it makes some virtues impracticable and others extremely difficult. Frugality is not only the basis of quiet, but of beneficence. No
man can help others that wants help himself; we must have enough
before we have to spare."

It is the bounden duty of every man to look his affairs in the face,
and to keep an account of his incomings and outgoings in money
matters. The exercise of a little simple arithmetic in this way will be
found of great value. Prudence requires that we shall pitch our scale
of living a degree below our means. But this can only be done by
carrying out faithfully a plan of living by which both ends may be
made to meet. John Locke strongly advised this course: "Nothing,"
said he, "is likelier to keep a man within compass than having con-

stantly before his eyes the state of his affairs in a regular course of account.'' The Duke of Wellington kept an accurate detailed account of all the money received and expended by him. Washington was very particular in matters of business and detail; and it is a remarkable fact, that he did not disdain to scrutinize the smallest outgoings of his household—determined as he was to live honestly within his means—even when holding the high office of President of the American Union.

Admiral Jervis has told the story of his early struggles, and, amongst other things, of his determination to keep out of debt. ''My father had a very large family,'' said he, ''with limited means. He gave me twenty pounds at starting, and that was all he ever gave me. After I had been a considerable time at the station I drew for twenty more, but the bill came back protested. I was mortified at this rebuke, and made a promise, which I have ever kept, that I would never draw another bill without a certainty of its being paid. I immediately changed my mode of living, quitted my mess, lived alone, and took up the ship's allowance, which I found quite sufficient; washed and mended my own clothes; made a pair of trousers out of the ticking of my bed; and having by these means saved as much money as would redeem my honor, I took up my bill, and from that time to this I have taken care to keep within my means.'' Jervis for six years endured pinching privation, but preserved his integrity, studied his profession with success, and gradually and steadily rose by merit and bravery to the highest rank. Middle-class people are too apt to live up to their incomes, if not beyond them, affecting a degree of ''style'' which is most unhealthy in its effects upon society at large. (*Happy Homes and the Hearts That Make Them* [Chicago: U.S. Publishing House, 1882], pp. 381–84.)

In another place Samuel Smiles shares a little-known fact about Demosthenes as a contrast to Cicero:

Yet Demosthenes, the eloquent, could be bought. When Harpalus, one of Alexander's chiefs, came to Athens, the orators had an eye upon his gold. Demosthenes was one of them. What is eloquence without honesty? On his visit to Harpalus, the chief perceived that Demosthenes was much pleased with one of the king's beautifully engraved cups. He desired him to take it in his hand that he might feel its weight. ''How much might it bring?'' asked Demosthenes. ''It will bring you twenty talents,'' replied Harpalus. That night the cup was sent to Demosthenes, with twenty talents in it. The present was not refused. The circumstance led to the disgrace of the orator, and he soon after poisoned himself. Cicero, on the other hand, refused all presents from friends, as well as from the enemies of his country.

Some time after his assassination, Caesar found one of his grandsons with a book of Cicero's in his hands. The boy endeavored to hide it, but Caesar took it from him. After having run over it, he returned it to the boy, saying, "My dear child, this was an eloquent man, and a lover of his country."

Freedom from debt is true freedom, as is freedom from sin. The Church has long had a policy of refusing federal funding so that no power or organization could force its ideologies and principles on the Church. There is some truth in the saying that those who hold the purse strings hold the power. There are frequently strings attached to gifts. If the Church would accept federal funding, then the government could force the Church to have atheistic teachers and to remove prayer and many other standards which this church is unwilling to accept.

Mission presidents have the opportunity of seeing the entire Church in miniature. They see the whole spectrum of the Church. There are a few missionaries who have absolutely no sense of responsibility at all regarding finances. To them, whatever they see they want and they buy it, knowing that Mom or Dad will cover. Some use the phone to the extent that hundreds of sacred dollars are wasted each month. Others are so used to "eating out" at home that they indulge themselves daily in the field. This can add a hundred or more dollars to mission costs each month.

The great missionaries learn to be Spartan. They know that every dollar used by a missionary in the field is sacred. They are frugal and careful. They budget monthly and live within the budget. The Lord blesses their sacrifice with success.

There are several principles I have often taught to missionaries and to newlyweds. Practice them all the days of your life and you will truly be free.

1. If you never buy anything you do not really need, you will never really need anything you cannot afford to buy. President N. Eldon Tanner referred to this as separating wants from needs.
2. President J. Reuben Clark, Jr., taught us that those who understand interest collect it and those who do not understand it pay it.

3. Do not spend tomorrow's dollars today. You will never be successful by using credit cards or borrowing against money that will come to you tomorrow.
4. Pay tithes and offerings.
5. Avoid debt as a plague.
6. Exercise a Spartan discipline in your life and eventually you will have an abundance.

Finally, my young friends, follow good, solid financial practices. Read great books on how to be successful. Then, when you see a measure of success and financial rewards, remember what Jacob taught in the Book of Mormon:

And now behold, my brethren, this is the word which I declare unto you, that many of you have begun to search for gold, and for silver, and for all manner of precious ores, in the which this land, which is a land of promise unto you and to your seed, doth abound most plentifully.

And the hand of providence hath smiled upon you most pleasingly, that you have obtained many riches; and because some of you have obtained more abundantly than that of your brethren ye are lifted up in the pride of your hearts, and wear stiff necks and high heads because of the costliness of your apparel, and persecute your brethren because ye suppose that ye are better than they.

And now, my brethren, do ye suppose that God justifieth you in this thing? Behold, I say unto you, Nay. But he condemneth you, and if ye persist in these things his judgments must speedily come unto you.

O that he would show you that he can pierce you, and with one glance of his eye he can smite you to the dust!

O that he would rid you from this iniquity and abomination. And, O that ye would listen unto the word of his commands, and let not this pride of your hearts destroy your souls!

Think of your brethren like unto yourselves, and be familiar with all and free with your substance, that they may be rich like unto you.

But before ye seek for riches, seek ye for the kingdom of God.

And after ye have obtained a hope in Christ ye shall obtain riches, if ye seek them; and ye will seek them for the intent to do good—to clothe the naked, and to feed the hungry, and to liberate the captive, and administer relief to the sick and the afflicted. (Jacob 2:12–19.)

Consider God's Servant Job

There was a man in the land of Uz, whose name was Job; and that man was perfect and upright, and one that feared God, and eschewed evil'' (Job 1:1). He had seven sons and three daughters. He was a man of great wealth and possessions. He owned seven thousand sheep, three thousand camels, five hundred yoke of oxen, five hundred mules, and a very great household, making him the greatest of all the men of the East. It appears that in nothing was Job deprived.

As is true from the foundation of the world, there will always be a spoiler—the great deceiver, the evil one, who wants to make all men like unto himself. He has no principles and no integrity. He is and ever will be a liar. There is no end to which he will not go, no evil which he will not commit to have power over men's souls.

Job became an object of his attention. Unquestionably Satan had tried to deceive and tempt Job throughout his life, but Job gave him no heed. Satan thought he could persuade God to withdraw the blessings that had come to Job as a result of his obedience to eternal principles.

The Lord, knowing Satan's evil intent, said, "Hast thou considered my servant Job, that there is none like him in the earth, a perfect and an upright man, one that feareth God, and escheweth evil?" (Job 1:8). Imagine having God refer to any man as "perfect and upright."

Nevertheless, Satan answered the Lord, "Doth Job fear God for nought?" And then Lucifer questioned the strength and source of Job's strength: "Hast not thou made an hedge about him, and about his house, and about all that he hath on every side? thou hast blessed the work of his hands, and his substance is increased in the land." (Job 1:9–10.)

Job was a wealthy man, and his greatest wealth was in his spirit. He was contented because he loved and served the Lord, and his spirit was at peace with God. His herds and flocks prospered and his children were obedient. His wealth was centered in spiritual blessings, and his earthly riches increased as well. Jealous Satan said to the Lord, "But put forth thine hand now, and touch all that he hath, and he will curse thee to thy face" (Job 1:11).

Satan understood the nature of man. He had watched man since the creation and had seen that often when reversals came to men's lives they accused God and abandoned their beliefs. Satan was confident that Job would do the same, but God knew Job's heart and had full confidence in him. "And the Lord said unto Satan, Behold, all that he hath is in thy power; only upon himself put not forth thine hand" (Job 1:12). The Lord knew that Job's wisdom and testimony were sufficient to know that possessions and riches were only things and may or may not be accumulated. Job also had an eternal perspective, and that would bring him through all these trials.

This great experience took place without Job knowing why he experienced these reversals and trials. Little did he know the extent to which he would be tested. If God had confided in him and shared what the test would be, Job would not have merited the same rewards. Somehow when you are aware of your test you know there will be a time limit and eventually relief and rewards will come. Job did not know.

Now notice what Satan does to all the good things of Job's life. Like the angry, wretched soul he is he destroys all that comes into his hands.

One day when Job's sons and daughters were eating and drinking wine in their eldest brother's house, four messengers came to Job, one after another, with tragic messages. Some of Job's servants were plowing the fields with oxen and the asses were feeding, and you will recall there were five hundred yoke of oxen and five hundred mules (asses). The animals were taken away by enemies and the servants were slain. Only the first servant alone escaped to bring Job this sad message. In our day that would be like wiping out a great segment of a man's wealth—and his ability to generate wealth. Saddest of all to Job was that his faithful servants had been slain. This news must have startled Job to the core of his being. I am confident that he had not recovered from this first message when the second servant came and announced a phenomenon which he accredited to God. "The fire of God is fallen from heaven, and hath burned up the sheep, and the servants, and consumed them; and I only am escaped alone to tell thee," reported the servant (Job 1:16). I would guess that Job's first thoughts focused on the wives and children of his servants whose lives had been taken.

Almost before this report had been given, a third servant reported that the Chaldeans, in three bands, had fallen on the three thousand camels, had taken them away, and had slain the servants. Only he had escaped to give Job this third traumatic message. One wonders why the shock alone did not bring about a heart attack or a stroke. Satan was taking advantage of the full limit of the Lord's agreement. In his evilness and nastiness, he sent a great wind from the wilderness and smote the four corners of the house, and it fell upon the seven sons of Job, killing them. The fourth servant brought this last message, which must have wrenched and crushed and broken Job's heart.

This is an easy story to read because we are not involved. It is happening to someone else and all we need to do is read a few more pages to see what the outcome will be. Try to comprehend what messages like those mentioned above would do to us. Job's emotions must have catapulted from one extreme to the other—

from shock, disbelief, outrage, grief, pain, agony, anger, and soul-sickness—all in only a few moments of time.

The scriptures state: "Then Job arose, and rent his mantle, and shaved his head, and fell down upon the ground, and [what? wept, cried, fainted, died? no, he] worshipped. And said, Naked came I out of my mother's womb, and naked shall I return thither: the Lord gave, and the Lord hath taken away; blessed be the name of the Lord." And the last verse of the first chapter of Job states, "In all this Job sinned not, nor charged God foolishly." (Job 1:20–22.)

We cannot comprehend the tender emotions and feelings which the God of heaven must have felt during these severe trials.

Job had proven his spiritual strength and Lucifer had proven how ruthless and totally evil he could be. Satan was not content to let the contest end here. In ages past he had known many others who had expressed their faith but who had faltered when their health was impaired. So Satan presented himself again before the Lord. The Lord said to him, "From whence comest thou?" Satan's response was that he had been "going to and fro in the earth, and from walking up and down in it." (Job 2:2.) He did not say what else he had been doing—tempting, afflicting, destroying, hurting, and working his evils and filthiness.

And a second time the Lord said to Lucifer, "Hast thou considered my servant Job, that there is none like him in the earth, a perfect and an upright man." And then the Lord, knowing Satan's thoughts, added, "And still he holdeth fast his integrity, although thou movedst me against him, to destroy him without cause." (Job 2:3.)

Satan was not content to lose this or any other contest in which he might be involved, either with Job or with any one of us. Addressing the Lord, Satan said: "Skin for skin, yea, all that a man hath will he give for his life. But put forth thine hand now, and touch his bone and his flesh, and he will curse thee to thy face" (Job 2:4–5).

And the Lord said, "Behold, he is in thine hand; but save his life" (Job 2:6). Again, consider the absolute confidence expressed by the Lord God Jehovah as Satan was given the freedom to further try Job. The Lord knew that Satan had no conscience, that he would do all in his power to destroy this faithful, good, upright man.

Job was "smote . . . with sore boils from the sole of his foot unto his crown." Boils are extremely painful. One or two would bring great pain and discomfort. Job was afflicted from head to foot. He took a "potsherd to scrape himself withal; and he sat down among the ashes."

Those around Job had not his great faith. Even his wife admonished him, "Dost thou still retain thine integrity? curse God, and die." (Job 2:7–9.) Having witnessed all that Job had been through and having equal or greater emotional involvement as she saw her seven sons slain, their riches dashed to pieces, and now her husband suffering beyond anything she had ever known, I suppose this good woman must have thought there was nothing left for which to live.

I have a young friend who has some severe emotional problems and she thinks there is nothing left in life but misery, sadness, and heartache.

Job's response to his wife might also be considered by my young friend. He said, "Thou speakest as one of the foolish women speaketh. What? shall we receive good at the hand of God, and shall we not receive evil?" Job's faith was simple and implicit. And the writer states, "In all this did not Job sin with his lips." (Job 2:10.)

Job had three friends who, after having heard of this evil, "came every one from his own place" (Job 2:11). They had come to mourn with him and comfort him. But the disfiguration of Job's features from the boils, the baldness from shaving his head, and the sackcloth and ashes made him unrecognizable. They saw him from "afar off, and knew him not." Like true friends "they lifted up their voice, and wept; and they rent every one his mantle, and sprinkled dust upon their heads toward heaven." (Job 2:12.) These three friends "sat down with him upon the ground seven days and seven nights, and none spake a word unto him: for they saw that his grief was very great" (Job 2:13).

There are some experiences in life that we go through, and no matter how great our vocabulary, words cannot express what we feel. Spirit must speak to spirit. These friends had come out of a need for an old, trusted friend and that was enough.

After this period of exquisite grief Job spoke. He cursed his day, that is the day he was born. So great was his suffering that he wished he had never been born. Also, he cried, "Why died I not from the womb?" (Job 3:11).

His friends made an attempt to talk to Job. They were concerned about his grief, but seven days of pondering and watching filled their hearts and minds. Eliphaz the Temanite exclaimed: "But who can withhold himself from speaking?" (Job 4:2). Then he reasoned with Job and counseled him because he mistakenly thought that Job had sinned. He discussed the Lord's mercy and goodness and that "happy is the man that God correcteth: . . . he maketh sore, and bindeth up: he woundeth, and his hands make whole . . . He shall redeem thee from death." (Job 5:17–18, 20.) He said many other things as well, but Job answered: "Oh that my grief were throughly weighed, and my calamity laid in the balances together! For now it would be heavier than the sand of the sea: therefore my words are swallowed up." (Job 6:2–3.) Job must have been considering his life and whether the weight of his sufferings was just.

Kahlil Gibran said, "The cavity created by the suffering through which we go becomes a receptacle for compensating blessings." I believe that is a true principle, one not understood by us and possibly questioned by Job at the height of his suffering.

The tragedies in Job's life give justification for a theological and philosophical discussion. He wonders whether there is an appointed time for man on the earth and why the Lord has not pardoned his transgressions. Even during all the discussions, Job only praises God, defends him, and honors him. And, finally a great soul-stirring declaration and testimony of his love for God: "Though he slay me, yet will I trust in him" (Job 13:15).

Once again a loving Heavenly Father must have been warmed by the love and faithfulness of Job. And later he offers words that have rung down through the centuries, first the ills that have befallen him and then his powerful, sacred witness:

He hath stripped me of my glory, and taken the crown from my head.

He hath destroyed me on every side, and I am gone: and mine hope hath he removed like a tree.

He hath also kindled his wrath against me, and he counteth me unto him as one of his enemies.

His troops come together, and raise up their way against me, and encamp round about my tabernacle.

He hath put my brethren far from me, and mine acquaintance are verily estranged from me.

My kinsfolk have failed, and my familiar friends have forgotten me.

They that dwell in mine house, and my maids, count me for a stranger: I am an alien in their sight. . . .

Yea, young children despised me; I arose, and they spake against me.

All my inward friends abhorred me: and they whom I loved are turned against me.

My bone cleaveth to my skin and to my flesh, and I am escaped with the skin of my teeth. (Job 19:9–15, 18–20.)

Then these thrilling words:

Oh that my words were now written! oh that they were printed in a book!

That they were graven with an iron pen and lead in the rock for ever!

For I know that my redeemer liveth, and that he shall stand at the latter day upon the earth:

And though after my skin worms destroy this body, yet in my flesh shall I see God:

Whom I shall see for myself, and mine eyes shall behold, and not another; though my reins be consumed within me. (Job 19:23–27.)

Job also learns that sometimes in life the wicked prosper, then he testifies that their judgment will come in a day of wrath and destruction. He recounts that murderers, adulterers, those who oppress the poor, and wicked people in general often go unpunished. (See chapter heading of Job 24, LDS edition of the Bible.)

Job eventually invites judgment so that God may know his integrity. It appears that this extreme suffering and grief have caused Job to focus on "charity," the pure love of Christ. This is often true with those who suffer. They become more empathetic towards those who suffer such great stress—the orphan, the widow, the poor, diseased, and sick. Now read these great words of a humble, penitent servant:

> If I have withheld the poor from their desire, or have caused the eyes of the widow to fail;
>
> Or have eaten my morsel myself alone, and the fatherless hath not eaten thereof;
>
> If I have seen any perish for want of clothing, or any poor without covering;
>
> If his loins have not blessed me, and if he were not warmed with the fleece of my sheep;
>
> If I have lifted up my hand against the fatherless, when I saw my help in the gate:
>
> Then let mine arm fall from my shoulder blade, and mine arm be broken from the bone. (Job 31:16–17, 19–22.)

These are the qualities that made Job a perfect and upright man in his generation.

The last chapter of Job describes the compensating blessings for suffering all things. Job repents in sackcloth and ashes and is vindicated before his friends. The Lord speaks to Eliphaz the Temanite and says, "My wrath is kindled against thee, and against thy two friends: for ye have not spoken of me the thing that is right, as my servant Job hath" (Job 42:7).

And the last verses in the book of Job state, "also the Lord gave Job twice as much as he had before":

> Then came there unto him all his brethren, and all his sisters, and all they that had been of his acquaintance before, and did eat bread with him in his house: and they bemoaned him, and comforted him over all the evil that the Lord had brought upon him: every man also gave him a piece of money, and every one an earring of gold.
>
> So the Lord blessed the latter end of Job more than his beginning: for he had fourteen thousand sheep, and six thousand camels, and a thousand yoke of oxen, and a thousand she asses.
>
> He had also seven sons and three daughters.
>
> And in all the land were no women found so fair as the daughters of Job: and their father gave them inheritance among their brethren.
>
> After this lived Job an hundred and forty years, and saw his sons, and his sons' sons, even four generations.
>
> So Job died, being old and full of days. (Job 42:11–13, 15–17.)

The life of Job can be a great comfort to each one of us as we face tests and trials in life—and we all will. President Harold B.

Lee said that we will be tested every month of our lives. He also stated that the "greatest trial we face in this life is the loss of a loved one" (*From the Valley of Despair to the Mountain Peaks of Hope,* [pamphlet, 1971]).

Death, divorce, not being able to have children, never marrying, broken friendships—all involve the loss of a loved one. Many have suffered through these tests. We may also be tried by the loss of a job, financial reverses, disobedient children, accidents, sickness, disease, pain, and all manner of sorrow.

Yet, we are not alone anymore than the Prophet Joseph was in Liberty Jail where it appears from his prayer that he felt abandoned by the Lord:

> O God, where art thou? And where is the pavilion that covereth thy hiding place?
>
> How long shall thy hand be stayed, and thine eye, yea thy pure eye, behold from the eternal heavens the wrongs of thy people and of thy servants, and thine ear be penetrated with their cries?
>
> Yea, O Lord, how long shall they suffer these wrongs and unlawful oppressions, before thine heart shall be softened toward them, and thy bowels be moved with compassion toward them?
>
> O Lord God Almighty, maker of heaven, earth, and seas, and of all things that in them are, and who controllest and subjectest the devil, and the dark and benighted dominion of Sheol—stretch forth thy hand; let thine eye pierce; let thy pavilion be taken up; let thy hiding place no longer be covered; let thine ear be inclined; let thine heart be softened, and thy bowels moved with compassion toward us.
>
> Let thine anger be kindled against our enemies; and, in the fury of thine heart, with thy sword avenge us of our wrongs.
>
> Remember thy suffering saints, O our God; and thy servants will rejoice in thy name forever.
>
> My son, peace be unto thy soul; thine adversity and thine afflictions shall be but a small moment;
>
> And then, if thou endure it well, God shall exalt thee on high; thou shalt triumph over all thy foes.
>
> Thy friends do stand by thee, and they shall hail thee again with warm hearts and friendly hands.
>
> Thou art not yet as Job; thy friends do not contend against thee, neither charge thee with transgressions, as they did Job. (D&C 121:1–10.)

After all these generations, the Lord in his great love and understanding reflects again on the life of his servant Job who was "perfect and upright in his generation."

Let his testimony be branded with a flaming fire on our hearts. Herein lies strength for the day:

> Oh that my words were now written! oh that they were printed in a book!
> That they were graven with an iron pen and lead in the rock for ever!
> For I know that my redeemer liveth, and that he shall stand at the latter day upon the earth:
> And though after my skin worms destroy this body, yet in my flesh shall I see God. (Job 19:23–26.)

We can be strengthened in times of our own trials if we prepare for them by considering God's servant Job, for he is a superb example to all youth and adults.

When Chaos Comes

There are threatening events in the future. We read of hurricanes, earthquakes, the possibility of nuclear holocaust, and other possible disasters. What does all of this mean to us who are members of the Church? What does it mean to you who are our youth?

Chaos suggests calamity, disorder, disorganization, destruction, disorientation, and so on. Consider these verses from Joseph Smith—Matthew as recorded in the Pearl of Great Price. They include the translation as revealed to Joseph Smith in 1831 of Matthew 23:39 and all of chapter 24:

> For I say unto you, that ye shall not see me henceforth and know that I am he of whom it is written by the prophets, until ye shall say: "Blessed is he who cometh in the name of the Lord, in the clouds of heaven, and all the holy angels with him. Then understood his disciples that he should come again on the earth, after that he was glorified and crowned on the right hand of God.
>
> And Jesus left them, and went upon the Mount of Olives. And as he sat upon the Mount of Olives, the disciples came unto him privately, saying: Tell us when shall these things be which thou hast said concerning the destruction of the temple, and the Jews; and

what is the sign of thy coming, and of the end of the world, or the destruction of the wicked, which is the end of the world?

And Jesus answered, and said unto them: Take heed that no man deceive you;

For many shall come in my name, saying—I am Christ—and shall deceive many;

Then shall they deliver you up to be afflicted, and shall kill you, and ye shall be hated of all nations, for my name's sake;

And then shall many be offended, and shall betray one another, and shall hate one another;

And many false prophets shall arise, and shall deceive many;

When you, therefore, shall see the abomination of desolation, spoken of by Daniel the prophet, concerning the destruction of Jerusalem, then you shall stand in the holy place; whoso readeth let him understand.

Then let them who are in Judea flee into the mountains;

Let him who is on the housetop flee, and not return to take anything out of his house;

Neither let him who is in the field return back to take his clothes;

And wo unto them that are with child, and unto them that give suck in those days;

Therefore, pray ye the Lord that your flight be not in the winter, neither on the Sabbath day;

For then, in those days; shall be great tribulation on the Jews, and upon the inhabitants of Jerusalem, such as was not before sent upon Israel, of God, since the beginning of their kingdom until this time; no, nor ever shall be sent again upon Israel.

For in those days there shall also arise false Christs, and false prophets, and shall show great signs and wonders, insomuch, that, if possible, they shall deceive the very elect, who are the elect according to the covenant.

Behold, I speak these things unto you for the elect's sake; and you also shall hear of wars, and rumors of wars; see that ye be not troubled, for all I have told you must come to pass; but the end is not yet.

And they shall hear of wars, and rumors of wars.

Behold I speak for mine elect's sake; for nation shall rise against nation, and kingdom against kingdom; there shall be famines, and pestilences, and earthquakes, in divers places.

And again, this Gospel of the Kingdom shall be preached in all the world, for a witness unto all nations, and then shall the end come, or the destruction of the wicked;

And immediately after the tribulation of those days, the sun shall be darkened, and the moon shall not give her light, and the stars shall fall from heaven, and the powers of heaven shall be shaken. (Joseph Smith—Matthew 1:1, 4, 5–9, 12–18, 22–23, 28–29, 31, 33.)

Now, verse 34 talks about a generation. I believe it is your generation.

Verily, I say unto you, this generation, in which these things shall be shown forth, shall not pass away until all I have told you shall be fulfilled.

Then, starting with verse 44:

Then shall be fulfilled that which is written, that in the last days, two shall be in the field, the one shall be taken, and the other left;

Two shall be grinding at the mill, the one shall be taken, and the other left;

And what I say unto one, I say unto all men; watch, therefore, for you know not at what hour your Lord doth come.

But know this, if the good man of the house had known in what watch the thief would come, he would have watched, and would not have suffered his house to have been broken up, but would have been ready.

Therefore be ye also ready, for in such an hour as ye think not, the Son of Man cometh.

Who, then, is a faithful and wise servant, whom his lord hath made ruler over his household, to give them meat in due season?

Blessed is that servant whom his lord, when he cometh, shall find so doing; and verily I say unto you, he shall make him ruler over all his goods. (Joseph Smith—Matthew 1:44–50.)

Now note, my beloved friends, what the Lord states in verse 11: "But he that remaineth steadfast and is not overcome, the same shall be saved."

We are expected to remain steadfast through trials. The Lord will not desert us. He will be faithful to his words.

Now let us look at other scriptures that give us further insight:

And it shall come to pass, because of the wickedness of the world, that I will take vengeance upon the wicked, for they will not repent; for the cup of mine indignation is full; for behold, my blood shall not cleanse them if they hear me not.

Wherefore, I the Lord God will send forth flies upon the face of the earth, which shall take hold of the inhabitants thereof, and shall eat their flesh, and shall cause maggots to come in upon them;

And their tongues shall be stayed that they shall not utter against me; and their flesh shall fall from off their bones, and their eyes from their sockets;

And it shall come to pass that the beasts of the forest and the fowls of the air shall devour them up.

And the great and abominable church, which is the whore of all the earth, shall be cast down by devouring fire, according as it is spoken by the mouth of Ezekiel the prophet, who spoke of these things, which have not come to pass but surely must, as I live, for abominations shall not reign. (D&C 29:17–21.)

In the second chapter of Joel we read these words:

A day of darkness and of gloominess, a day of clouds and of thick darkness, as the morning spread upon the mountains: a great people and a strong; there hath not been ever the like, neither shall be any more after it, even to the years of many generations.

A fire devoureth before them; and behind them a flame burneth: the land is as the garden of Eden before them, and behind them a desolate wilderness; yea, and nothing shall escape them.

The appearance of them is as the appearance of horses; and as horsemen, so shall they run.

Like the noise of chariots on the tops of mountains shall they leap, like the noise of a flame of fire that devoureth the stubble, as a strong people set in battle array.

Before their face the people shall be much pained: all faces shall gather blackness. (Joel 2:2–6, 10.)

Always the Lord has his promise for those who are obedient. What comfort we receive from the scriptures.

Therefore also now, saith the Lord, turn ye even to me with all your heart, and with fasting, and with weeping, and with mourning:

And rend your heart, and not your garments, and turn unto the Lord your God: for he is gracious and merciful, slow to anger, and of great kindness, and repenteth him of the evil.

Gather the people, sanctify the congregation, assemble the elders, gather the children, and those that suck the breasts: let the bridegroom go forth of his chamber, and the bride out of her closet.

Let the priests, the ministers of the Lord, weep between the porch and the altar, and let them say, Spare thy people, O Lord, and give not thine heritage to reproach, that the heathen should rule over them: wherefore should they say among the people, Where is their God?

Then will the Lord be jealous for his land, and pity his people.

Yea, the Lord will answer and say unto his people, Behold, I will send you corn, and wine, and oil, and ye shall be satisfied therewith: and I will no more make you a reproach among the heathen:

But I will remove far off from you the northern army, and will drive him into a land barren and desolate, with his face toward the east sea, and his hinder part toward the utmost sea, and his stink shall come up, and his ill savour shall come up, because he hath done great things.

Fear not, O land; be glad and rejoice: for the Lord will do great things. (Joel 2:12–13, 16–21.)

The Lord will do great things. We will see his righteous judgment come upon those who reject his words, who delight in abominations, who trespass on sacred grounds. The Lord is long-suffering but, as in all things, time does run out.

Let us refer to a few selected verses from Revelation and then discuss what we should do. There are occurrences that will take place during the sixth seal (six thousandth year) and the seventh seal, or the millennium prior to the Lord's second coming.

And I beheld when he had opened the sixth seal, and, lo, there was a great earthquake; and the sun became black as sackcloth of hair, and the moon became as blood;

And the stars of heaven fell unto the earth, even as a fig tree casteth her untimely figs, when she is shaken of a mighty wind.

And the heaven departed as a scroll when it is rolled together; and every mountain and island were moved out of their places. (Revelation 6:12–14.)

And in Revelation, chapter 16:

And there were voices, and thunders, and lightnings; and there was a great earthquake, such as was not since men were upon the earth, so mighty an earthquake, and so great.

And the great city was divided into three parts, and the cities of the nations fell: and great Babylon came in remembrance before God, to give unto her the cup of the wine of the fierceness of his wrath.

And every island fled away, and the mountains were not found.

And there fell upon men a great hail out of heaven, every stone about the weight of a talent: and men blasphemed God because of the plague of the hail; for the plague thereof was exceeding great. (Revelation 16:18–21.)

And then during the seventh seal: "And in those days shall men seek death, and shall not find it; and shall desire to die, and death shall flee from them" (Revelation 9:6).

And then also regarding the two "witnesses" (prophets of the Lord):

And I will give power unto my two witnesses, and they shall prophesy a thousand two hundred and threescore days, clothed in sackcloth.

These are the two olive trees, and the two candlesticks standing before the God of the earth.

And if any man will hurt them, fire proceedeth out of their mouth, and devoureth their enemies: and if any man will hurt them, he must in this manner be killed.

These have power to shut heaven, that it rain not in the days of their prophecy: and have power over waters to turn them to blood, and to smite the earth with all plagues, as often as they will.

And when they shall have finished their testimony, the beast that ascendeth out of the bottomless pit shall make war against them, and shall overcome them, and kill them.

And their dead bodies shall lie in the street of the great city, which spiritually is called Sodom and Egypt, where also our Lord was crucified.

And they of the people and kindreds and tongues and nations shall see their dead bodies three days and a half, and shall not suffer their dead bodies to be put in graves.

And they that dwell upon the earth shall rejoice over them, and make merry, and shall send gifts one to another; because these two prophets tormented them that dwelt on the earth.

And after three days and an half the Spirit of life from God entered into them, and they stood upon their feet; and great fear fell upon them which saw them.

And they heard a great voice from heaven saying unto them, Come up hither. And they ascended up to heaven in a cloud; and their enemies beheld them. (Revelation 11:3–12.)

These are exciting times. Do not worry, but stand in holy places. The rewards are certain and the prophecies are true.

And I heard a great voice out of heaven saying, Behold, the tabernacle of God is with men, and he will dwell with them, and they shall be his people, and God himself shall be with them, and be their God.

And God shall wipe away all tears from their eyes; and there shall be no more death, neither sorrow, nor crying, neither shall there be any more pain: for the former things are passed away. (Revelation 21:3–4.)

Then note the conditions in which we shall live if we are faithful.

And the twelve gates were twelve pearls; every several gate was of one pearl: and the street of the city was pure gold, as it were transparent glass.

And I saw no temple therein; for the Lord God Almighty and the Lamb are the temple of it.

And the city had no need of the sun, neither of the moon, to shine in it: for the glory of God did lighten it, and the Lamb is the light thereof.

And the nations of them which are saved shall walk in the light of it: and the kings of the earth do bring their glory and honour into it.

And the gates of it shall not be shut at all by day: for there shall be no night there.

And they shall bring the glory and honour of the nations into it.

And there shall in no wise enter into it any thing that defileth, neither whatsoever worketh abomination, or maketh a lie: but they which are written in the Lamb's book of life. (Revelation 21:21–27.)

Also in Revelation, chapter 22:

And they shall see his face; and his name shall be in their foreheads.

And there shall be no night there; and they need no candle, neither light of the sun; for the Lord God giveth them light: and they shall reign for ever and ever.

And he said unto me, These sayings are faithful and true: and the Lord God of the holy prophets sent his angel to shew unto his servants the things which must shortly be done.

Behold, I come quickly: blessed is he that keepeth the sayings of the prophecy of this book.

Blessed are they that do his commandments, that they may have right to the tree of life, and may enter in through the gates into the city. (Revelation 22:4–7, 14.)

You may not understand or tie together all these things. However, all suggest the preparation that should take place in our lives. The following points help clarify the above scriptures and can be beneficial to our lives if practiced.

Obedience

We must be obedient. Remember that obedience brings freedom and disobedience brings bondage. Obedience is doing what the Lord has commanded us to do because it is the very best way of all the possible alternatives. If we are obedient, the Lord knows that our souls are not rebellious. If we are to be spared, we must be obedient.

Trust in the Lord

Confidence in the Lord comes through serving him and our fellowman. We know that we can turn to him during our trials and that somehow he will make us equal to the test. Realizing that he is our spiritual Father is enough, for the believer, to cause us to love him. His promises are sure. He will not forget his covenant children, so we need not fear the distressing days ahead. In fact, they are necessary for the fulfillment of all his promises.

Keep the Commandments

Through modern prophets we have been counseled to do many things that will prepare us for the future:

Pray with all our hearts in secret and with our families.

Study the scriptures daily.

Hold quality family home evenings.

Live worthy of our membership in the Church of Jesus Christ.

Have a year's supply of food and necessities.

Stay out of debt. This is especially true of young couples just starting families.

Do not cross over the line of propriety. That is, avoid R-rated movies, pornography, drugs, profanity, dirty stories, lying, cheating, and so forth.

Take care of your clothes, homes, equipment, and such items so that they will have an extended life. This will save you untold dollars and grief. Paint and renew those things that are costly.

Learn to do repair work that is costly if hired out.

Be spiritual, be happy, be excited, and get appropriate exercise.

My friends, you do not need to fear what Satan or his agents on this earth can do. The power behind us when we are obedient and pure is far greater than any work that Lucifer can bring to pass. We may be outnumbered, we may not make the progress we would like, but when the summer is over, the harvest ended, this work will be victorious.

Determine as a family what each of you would do should a calamity come while you are away from home. Decide where your family will meet—determine a time after the calamity: four hours, four days, or some other amount of time. Determine how you would get in touch if you are separated. Think of all of the possible things that could occur and then determine a plan for your family.

Consider such things as: power outage; earthquake destruction and your home; fire; injury; winds, cold, rain, snow; mode of travel—car (fuel), bike, horse; welfare of extended family—how to get in touch; radio broadcasts; neighbors with special professional skills; a 72-hour emergency pack.

Consider all of these plus the myriad other possibilities. Discuss them as a family. Determine a plan of action. Any plan is better than no plan, which generally results in chaos.

Be positive about living in this day. Partake of it to the fullest. It is my belief that most of us desired to come to the earth during this very "season." We knew what would be expected, and I imagine when we were told that we would be assigned to come to the earth to assist in ushering in the great millennial reign, our excitement could hardly be contained. I also believe that God trusted us to come at this time. You probably passed the word along about your particular assignment to earth in the same way a missionary does who reads his letter and tells the family, "I am going to the greatest mission in the world—the Texas San Antonio Mission." (At least that is how our family felt about my assignment to preside over that mission.)

There must have been some special preparation, some expert training, and some inspired counseling—the most profound of which was to trust in God, have faith, and be prepared.

Walk in the light of the Lord. Do not let satanic designs obscure your mission. Every one of you has a divine commission for which you will be accountable. You have been selected from the myriad souls who are our Father's spiritual children to walk on the earth during the dispensation of the fulness of times.

You will witness this great church moving with all its power and majesty. You will be able to observe the Apostles and prophets fulfilling their destiny of testifying before presidents, rulers of nations, and before all people. You will live to see their prophecies fulfilled.

God bless you. Be prepared but do not fear. When chaos comes you will be ready. Remember the sweet words of Jesus to those of us in this church who are faithful.

Therefore, fear not, little flock; do good; let earth and hell combine against you, for if ye are built upon my rock, they cannot prevail.

Behold, I do not condemn you; go your ways and sin no more; perform with soberness the work which I have commanded you.

Look unto me in every thought; doubt not, fear not.

Behold the wounds which pierced my side, and also the prints of the nails in my hands and feet; be faithful, keep my commandments, and ye shall inherit the kingdom of heaven. Amen. (D&C 6:34–37.)

"Fear Not, Little Flock"

Just after the turn of the century, Brother Cobbley was out cleaning his yard. He had a large pitchfork in his hands. Someone had discarded a large gunnysack in his flower bed and he thought it was filled with refuse. He was about to pick the sack and contents up with the pitchfork when he heard a small cry issue forth from this old burlap sack. He looked inside and saw a little infant girl, perhaps a few hours old.

The Cobbleys had twelve children, one of whom had recently been killed. Sister Cobbley had grieved deeply over the loss of this son. Brother Cobbley took this little girl inside and the whole family called her their "gift from God." They adopted this wonderful little soul. She grew up in that marvelous Latter-day Saint home in the sweet community of Pleasant Grove, Utah. She was always vivacious, warm, friendly, and considerate of everyone. She was very selective in choosing a marriage partner and found a young man whom she thought was a man destined to do great things. The little girl was a gift from God but her life represented a gift of God. Her husband became a bishop, a stake president, a temple president, and a General Authority. She is the eternal companion of Elder O. Leslie Stone.

We do not know what trials and challenges many of our closest friends have had. A few days ago my son Paul and I were reading the Book of Mormon together. We were at the part in 1 Nephi in which Nephi had broken his steel bow and thus the family had no way to obtain food. I said to Paul: "Nephi's brothers complained and griped. They were angry and murmured constantly. Not one of them thought of a solution of how to work out the problem." Then I said to Paul, "But do you know what Nephi did?" And he responded, "Suffered in silence."

Many people quietly go through this life suffering in silence. We recently buried my mother. After the funeral, family members were going through her possessions. There are six boys and two girls in our family. One brother is deceased. As I thought about these old possessions, I considered my mother's lonely life. My father became an alcoholic—I think even before he and Mother married. At that time she was a nonmember. Through the following years she was lonely, heartsick, and heavily burdened.

Could it be possible that through our righteous works, sacrifice, time, commitment, and faith in the Master that somehow he would be merciful to our children and wayward parents as well? I truly hope so.

My mother died on a Thursday night at eight-thirty, and the following day I went to Florida for a stake conference. The funeral was to be Monday after I returned. I did not share my mother's passing with the stake until the last few minutes of the general session.

There was a young missionary who had not fulfilled his calling faithfully and who had been involved in indiscretions so serious that I had to make a decision as to whether he should stay in the mission field or return home. He wanted to stay, but he did not seem repentant or sincere. I said to him, "Is your father active in the Church?" He replied that he was not. "How about your mother?" "Yes, she is the stake Young Women president."

We talked for a long while and then I said to him, "I am going to let you stay on your mission, but not because of you. It's because a wonderful mother has great confidence that her son will be an excellent missionary, and you will never know how much it would hurt her to see her son sent home dishonorably from his mission."

The following day, after I spoke about the passing of my

mother and shared the love which I have always had for her, this young missionary came up to me after the session. Tears were washing down his cheeks and he said: "I'm sorry about your mother. Now I know why you are letting me stay; you do not want to hurt my mother." Then he hugged me and said, "I will be a good missionary and never embarrass my mother."

The righteous plea of a mother rings out across the miles, "Oh, where is my wandering boy tonight?" and his love for her brings him back home.

A sweet sister recently stood up in stake conference to speak. She stated that they had a large family, and in essence said this: "We have been preparing our oldest son for a mission ever since he was a child. When he turned twelve, we bought him his missionary scriptures. Each year we did subtle things that would point him in the direction of a mission. When he turned seventeen he said, 'I do not think I will serve a mission.' " His folks responded that they hoped he would go, because President Kimball had said that every young man is expected to go on a mission. The Lord wanted him to go but it was his decision, they would not force him.

They said: "If you go on a mission, we will pay your mission expenses if you will earn enough money to get you into the mission field—buy all your clothes and the other materials and pay your travel costs to the Missionary Training Center." The grandparents had agreed to take care of the young man's expenses while in the MTC.

When this fine young man neared his nineteenth birthday, the bishop called him in and interviewed him for worthiness, and on behalf of the Lord extended a call to serve a mission. After the interview, he went home excitedly and told his parents he had accepted a call to serve a mission.

At that time the mother and father did not have the resources nor the necessary income to pay for their son's mission. This good woman knelt down the next day and said: "Heavenly Father, our son has accepted a mission call. He has his money, his grandparents are prepared to help, but we do not have any money to pay for his mission as we promised. Please show us how or help us find some way of earning the money to support this missionary. We will do anything.''

The next day the phone rang; it was a woman from the Newspaper Agency Corporation. She said to this good woman: "You know a lot of people out in that area. We have four *Tribune* and four *Deseret News* paper routes open and we need several people to carry them.'' The mother thought about her prayer and said, "We will take all eight routes.''

She and some of her children get up at 3:00 A.M. and fold the papers, then they deliver them until about 7:00 A.M. The children go to school and hurry home so they can help their mom fold the papers and deliver them until about 7:00 P.M.

How could a missionary be anything but great knowing that his mother and brothers and sisters were up at 3:00 A.M. to support him on his mission. How could he ever sleep in past 6:30 A.M. knowing his mom had been up several hours before. I promise you there are angels accompanying that little family every morning and night as they support a missionary.

The Lord promised in section 84, verse 88, of the Doctrine and Covenants: "For I will go before your face. I will be on your right hand and on your left, and my Spirit shall be in your hearts, and mine angels round about you, to bear you up"—and your family also, I might add.

Some years ago not too far from Salt Lake City, I organized a stake. We interviewed all of the members of the stake presidency, the bishops, and the high council. One fine brother's name kept coming to our attention. When we interviewed him he had been in the Church a relatively short few years. We asked if he had ever been involved in a major transgression. He said, "Not since I was baptized." We told him that it was one thing to forgive a person and another thing to place him on a pedestal. We said, "We need to know if there was a problem before baptism." There had been. He had committed a serious transgression repeatedly. He had stopped living an unfaithful life to his companion. He knew it was not right. Years later the missionaries came and he and his family believed and were baptized. Upon joining the Church, he labored with all his heart, as if he were trying to make up for lost time. He became an elders quorum president, a bishop, a high councilor, and served in many other callings. Now he was being considered as a member of the stake presidency. After he was excused from our presence, we continued to interview others. His name came up quite often. He was loved by his brethren. Each time his name would come up my mind would go back to the series of transgressions which I knew were abominable before the Lord.

Finally, toward the end of our interviews, a fine young high councilor came in. He recommended this man we had been discussing and I asked him, "Why would he be your first choice?" And he replied, "Because he is the cleanest, purest man I have ever met and it shows in his face." Tears welled up in my eyes and a great peace came into my bosom and in my heart. I thought: "Vaughn Featherstone, you know better. When a man is washed clean through the blood of the Lamb, he is clean, and the Lord said, 'I will remember his sins no more.' " This fine man was called as the presiding authority in that stake.

Victor Hugo wrote in his great work *Les Miserables,* "The shepherd does not recoil from the diseased sheep." He gently heals them and then they are without spot.

A wonderful couple came to my office recently. They had had financial problems that seemed to bury them. The man had worked for a dishonest employer who had cheated them out of several thousand dollars. This young couple became desperate and turned to the Lord. The husband said to the wife: "Let us exercise faith. We are going to give every penny we have to the Lord and then we can call on him for blessings." They were already full-tithe payers. Unbeknown to her husband, the wife had saved $157 which she was going to use to visit her daughter at Ricks College. Her husband was not aware of this money and she thought it should not be included.

They went through her purse and his wallet. They retrieved the bottle of coins, mostly pennies, and put them in paper rolls. Then, they waited for Sunday to contribute this money, every single penny, to the Lord. The woman said later that she worried about the Ricks College travel money. Two days passed and she said that she went and got the money and gave it to her husband to give to the Lord. Sunday they carried a bag containing now every single cent they had in this world. Knowing their circumstances, the bishop was humbled to the dust of the earth. Within the week, a man handed this good brother a one hundred dollar bill and said that he had felt impressed to give it to him. Another man gave them a check for thirty dollars to pay for gasoline to a leadership training conference. Also, within the week another man handed him a check for two thousand dollars "to help him out."

This good brother, who had such great faith, established a business and may well have made a fifty thousand–dollar income last year. The Lord knows; the Lord cares; the Lord fulfills his promises.

Many years ago I served as a priest quorum adviser in Boise. One of the young men with whom I worked was Ronald Loveland. Ron Loveland went on a mission to Uruguay and served under President J. Thomas Fyans. Years after his mission, Elder Loveland was called as the president of the Texas San Antonio Mission. Can you imagine the privilege that was mine to be called to succeed Ronald Loveland as president of that mission? My, what a thrill to see how the missionaries loved their wonderful, young mission president! His whole life has been committed to building the kingdom.

At a mission reunion last April, President Loveland spoke. He told of this experience from his mission to Uruguay.

One morning he and his companion were about to leave the apartment in Menes, Uruguay. There came a firm knock at the door. Elder Loveland answered and an eleven-year-old boy, barefooted with only a shirt and overalls, was standing at the door. he said, "Tell me what you believe." Elder Loveland turned to his companion and said: "The president said we needed men in the Church, that we are to search for families to teach. I guess we shouldn't teach him." His companion said, "I guess we should." They had this young man come in and they taught him a discussion. He came back every day to hear the following discussions. Finally, when the last discussion had been taught, this young man believed and wanted to be baptized. The missionaries said, "We will have to get your parent's permission." He said: "I do not have any parents. When I was two or three my parents abandoned me. A neighbor, who had a large family, took me in. They said, 'We have many mouths to feed, one more will not make any difference.' " The Elders said: "We will need to get their permission to baptize you. Take us to your home." The boy lived five miles out in the country. He had walked five miles into Menes, Uruguay, had gone from door to door asking where the Mormon missionaries lived, and then, upon finding them, had knocked on the door and said, "Tell me what you believe."

The missionaries walked out into the country and talked to this young man's foster parents and asked for permission to baptize him into the Church. They responded that the boy could do anything he wanted, that he only lived with them.

They baptized this young man and somehow over the next few weeks saved enough pesos to buy him an old, used bike. Then, instead of walking the five miles to church every Sunday he would pump his bike. He was ordained a deacon and was assigned to bring a man confined to a wheelchair to church. The boy would ride to church on his bike, lean it up against the chapel, then walk the three blocks to the home of the man in the wheelchair. He would push him to church, then attend to his duties of passing the sacrament. After church he would push his friend back home, walk back to church, and ride his bike home.

The missionaries were transferred out of Menes, Uruguay, and that was the last time Ron Loveland ever saw his young, convert friend.

Years later President Loveland's son Brad was called on a mission. He was assigned by a prophet of God to labor in Uruguay. Brad was pleased to follow his noble father. When he arrived in the field the president of the mission assigned him to his first field of labor, Menes, Uruguay. The bishop asked him and his companion to go out and attempt to reactivate those who had been baptized in the past but who were now inactive. He gave the Elders the names of active Saints who could help them locate the inactives.

One day Elder Loveland and his companion were in the home of one of the stake high councilors. They were visiting with the wife when the husband came home from work. The wife introduced the missionaries to her husband. The father looked startled when he heard Elder Loveland's name and asked, "By any chance, did you have an uncle or a relative who served down here about twenty years ago?" And Elder Loveland said, "Yes, my father." Then this wonderful high councilor went to Elder Loveland and embraced him and said that he was the eleven-year-old boy who had walked five miles into town to find out about the Church.

"I will be on your right hand and on your left."

In the sixth section of the Doctrine and Covenants, the Lord said:

> Fear not to do good, my sons, for whatsoever ye sow, that shall ye also reap; therefore, if ye sow good ye shall also reap good for your reward.
>
> Therefore, fear not, little flock; do good; let earth and hell combine against you, for if ye are built upon my rock, they cannot prevail.
>
> Behold, I do not condemn you; go your ways and sin no more; perform with soberness the work which I have commanded you.
>
> Look unto me in every thought; doubt not, fear not.
>
> Behold the wounds which pierced my side, and also the prints of the nails in my hands and feet; be faithful, keep my commandments, and ye shall inherit the kingdom of heaven. Amen. (D&C 6:33–37.)

I testify to you, this work is built on his rock. I further testify that if we heed his word and help in his work our hearts will echo the consoling phrase, "Fear not, little flock."

PART THREE

PREPARE FOR
THE FUTURE

CHAPTER SEVENTEEN

An Age of Wonder

In 1901 Wilbur and Orville Wright sold the first airplane to the government. They received a five-thousand-dollar award. It flew ten miles in fifteen minutes. On May 20, 1927, Charles Lindbergh climbed into the "Spirit of St. Louis." Everyone expected him to fly transcontinentally. Instead of banking the plane to the west, he banked it out over the Atlantic ocean. He faced winds and storms and dense fogs. Thirty-three hours and thirty minutes after takeoff, he landed at Le Bourget field in France. He became an international hero. The whole world wondered how he had accomplished this magnificent feat alone.

A New York newspaper writer penned these words in tribute to Lindbergh. I have taken the occasion to memorize them because they are so impressive.

> Alone? Is he alone, at whose right side rides courage, who has skill sitting within the cockpit and faith upon his left hand? What is solitude to him who has self-reliance to show the way and ambition to read the dials? Does he lack for company for whom the air is cleft by daring, and darkness is made light by enterprise? True, the bodies of other men are absent from his crowded cabin, but as his aircraft keeps its course, he holds communion with those rarer spirits whose sustaining potency gives strength to his arm, resourcefulness to his

mind, and contentment to his soul. Alone? With what more inspiring companions could he fly? ("Alone?" *New York Sun,* May 21, 1927.)

Stake President Mason in the Redmond Washington Stake is a test pilot. He has flown at heights so great that they are still classified information. I know of flights in excess of 90,000 feet in the air. Imagine the sensation of traveling at speeds of nearly three thousand miles an hour and at heights never dreamed of.

John Gillespie Magee, Jr., put into poetry the feelings generated by his own experience:

High Flight

Oh! I have slipped the surly bonds of earth
    And danced the skies on laughter-silvered wings;
Sunward I've climbed, and joined the tumbling mirth
    Of sun-split clouds—and done a hundred things
You have not dreamed of—wheeled and soared and swung
    High in the sunlit silence, hov'ring there.
I've chased the shouting wind alone, and flung
    My eager craft through footless halls of air.

Up, up the long delirious burning blue
    I've topped the wind-swept heights with easy grace
Where never lark, nor even eagle flew—
    And while with silent lifting mind I've trod
The high untrespassed sanctity of space,
    Put out my hand and touched the face of God.

We live in the period of man's most monumental achievements scientifically, and still we stand as pygmies in the things that pertain to God. Jacob, the brother of Nephi, exclaimed: "O that cunning plan of the evil one! O the vainness, and the frailties, and the foolishness of men! When they are learned they think they are wise, and they hearken not unto the counsel of God, for they set it aside, supposing they know of themselves, wherefore, their wisdom is foolishness and it profiteth them not. And they shall perish. But to be learned is good if they hearken unto the counsels of God." (2 Nephi 9:28–29.)

President Spencer W. Kimball said that the knowledge of man compared to God's knowledge is as a grain of sand to the Rock of

Gilbraltar. We live in a time in which man has walked on the moon, probed millions of light years into the cosmos, discovered cures for nearly every major disease, and invented an artificial heart.

At the same time, enemies of freedom have never been more open, more mocking, or more blatant in their quest for world domination and the enslavement of men's minds.

In this ruthless age of aggression, there is a quiet, holy people who have a destiny like no other generation. Let me share with you what that divine destiny will be.

In a stake in southern California a youth dance was held. A contract for the dance had been given to a musical group. It was written in the contract that the sound level would not exceed ninety-seven decibels. The decorations were special, the lighting was appropriate, and the young people from the local stakes were well groomed. Then the "combo" arrived. There were several shaggy-looking individuals in dirty Levi's. The leader had his shirt open in the front halfway down his chest—no hair grew there, but the shirt was nonetheless open. They put together their sound system, including large amplifiers. Then they started to play. The band leader had turned the volume up full blast.

At the end of the first number the high councilor adviser chaperoning the dance went to the leader and asked him to turn the music down to ninety-seven decibels as agreed on in the contract. The band leader refused. "This is the way the young people want it," he said, "and this is the way they are going to get it." The high councilor said: "Fine. You can pack up all your equipment and leave. We are not going to pay you unless you turn the music down." The young man responded, "We're going to stay, and you are going to pay us, and we are going to play the way the youth want it."

How about that? A group of scroungy, shaggy musicians trying to tell us what the standard will be in the Church of Jesus Christ.

Right in the middle of this confrontation, about a half-dozen priests from the stake came over to the stage. They said to the band leader, "You do what our high councilor told you to do." The music was turned down to the level of ninety-seven decibels.

This is a great story in a seemingly not too serious setting, but with very serious implications. We do have special standards as members of The Church of Jesus Christ of Latter-day Saints. It is thrilling to see youth uphold these standards.

In 1844, Dennison Harris and Robert Scott were invited by a member of the First Presidency, William Law, to come to his home. Dennison Harris was the son of Emer, a nephew of Martin Harris. These two young men went to Emer Harris to find out what they should do. Emer told them to go see the Prophet Joseph and do exactly what he told them to do. They did this. Joseph told them to go to the meeting, find out who was there, and what the purpose of the meeting was. They went to the meeting. There was an armed guard at the door. He let the two boys in. They were both seventeen—priest age.

There were in the meeting the Foster brothers, the Higbee brothers, Wilson Law, an apostate and brother of William, and other apostates. The purpose of the meeting was to determine how to murder Joseph and Hyrum to remove them from this earth.

The two boys reported all this to Joseph. He told them to go to each succeeding meeting. The first meeting was held on the last Sunday of March 1844. Four weeks later, the boys for some reason went to see Joseph before the meeting. He said to them: "Boys, this will be their last meeting. They will not meet again. Go to the meeting, but if they ask you to take any oaths or covenants do not, even at the peril of your life. They may attempt to do you harm, but I think they will not." He went on to say, "But, boys, if they do try to take your lives, stand up and die like men and you will die a martyr's death, but I think they will not. If anyone attempts to do you any harm [and I love him for this], I will come and stand as a lion in their path."

The boys went to the meeting. This time there were two guards at the door and they were not about to let Dennison Harris and Robert Scott in. Finally, the young men prevailed upon the guards and were permitted inside. The house was filled with men. The young men went back in a corner against a wall where they were inconspicuous. During the meeting every man was to come to a table in the central part of the room. A clerk sat at the table and a Justice of the Peace stood behind it. Everyone would sign his name and then take the oath: "I covenant and promise before God and all his holy angels that I will use every particle of influence I have and never cease striving until this earth is rid of Joseph and Hyrum Smith. So help me God."

After everyone had taken the oath except Dennison Harris and Robert Scott, they suddenly became very conspicuous. They were brought to the table and ordered to take the oath and sign the papers. Pale, trembling, fearful as we ever are in life, the two young men said, "No, we will never take the oath." Knives and swords were drawn and placed at their throats. They felt rifle barrels thrust against their backs. One of the boys said that he felt a trigger click back. The leader said to the boys: "Either you take the oath or you die this instant. You know too much to ever leave here alive." A second time, these two young men said, "We will not take the oath." The evil men were about to do them in when someone standing by the door said: "You are making too much noise. People can hear you out in the street."

They took these young men down into the cellar. Everyone gathered around. Knives were placed at their throats, swords hung over their heads, and rifles in their backs. The leader said: "Boys, this is your last chance. Either you take the oath or you die." A third time, pale and trembling, they said, "No, we will never take the oath."

One account says that a sword was starting to fall on one of the boys, when a man on the stairs said: "We'd better think this through. Undoubtedly Emer knows where his boy is, and if we do him any harm great mischief may befall us." They talked it over and turned Dennison Harris and Robert Scott free with this oath, "If you so much as divulge one word that was spoken here, we will hunt you down and kill you, so help us God."

The first person the two boys met after they were turned loose was Joseph. "Remember," he had said, "if anyone attempts to harm you, I will come and stand as a lion in his path." He was concerned about the boys and had come looking for them.

He took them to a secluded spot behind his home and sat on a log with them. He had them rehearse all that had happened and was moved to tears at what they told him. What love for the Prophet, what bravery, what integrity!

"O then, my beloved brethren, come unto the Lord, the Holy One. Remember that his paths are righteous. Behold, the way for man is narrow, but it lieth in a straight course before him, and the keeper of the gate is the Holy One of Israel; and he employeth no servant there; and there is none other way save it be by the gate; for he cannot be deceived, for the Lord God is his name." (2 Nephi 9:41.)

Surely it is a marvel that man can fly to unthinkable heights and at tremendous speeds. No less of a marvel is it that young men's souls can reach to unfathomable depths of commitment to the restored gospel of Jesus Christ.

A flood of knowledge and truth began when the Father and the Son appeared to Joseph Smith. An age of wonder began that constitutes the restoration of all things since the beginning of mortality. We are called to become part of that wonder and stead-fastly follow the straight course leading to "the keeper of the gate," even "the Holy One of Israel." Let us be diligent in seeking out the ways of the Lord.

Seeing into the Future

Someone has said that prophecy is history backwards. How would you like to see into the future and see what would happen to your school friends, your church peer group, and your neighbors? You can know, not from actual predestination but from the past. Let me share with you some examples by way of personal experience. I will give you the profile of several people I knew as a high school student and what has happened to them.

Years ago a young man transferred to our school from another school. Both of us had one thing in common, so automatically I had an interest in him. We were not close friends but we had several classes together. I remember catching him cheating by reading my answers to a test. I do not cheat and I have always resented the act of those who do. We had a confrontation and I told him that I thought he was a better man than to cheat. We were not close so I only came in contact with him a few times in the next thirty years.

He came to see me as a General Authority and reminded me of this incident. I had forgotten it. During our visit he introduced me to his "new" wife (a second marriage). He showed me something he had constructed and was selling for two thousand dollars. He had several exhibits handy. I took the couple to lunch and visited at length with them.

Later that day while I was visiting with a local car dealer, one of his salesmen came into the office and said that he had just interviewed this same man. The man had told the salesman that I was buying several of these items that he was selling for two thousand dollars each. I said: "Is he still there? I want to talk to him because he is lying." First, I could not afford his items, and second, I questioned their value.

This man was using my name as a General Authority to trade his items for a new car. In addition to the great misuse of my name, he had lied. He had developed the sinful habit of dishonesty in high school and had apparently never repented of that sin.

A beautiful girl who went to school with us was equally as beautiful on the inside. She was a school officer all three years in high school. She was always modest in her dress, fair complected, and blonde—altogether a lovely woman. No one ever criticized her to my knowledge. She was an excellent student, selective about the company she kept, and always active in the Church. She went on to the University of Utah, where she met her husband. She is as lovely today as she was then. I served as junior and senior class presidents so we were in school government (Board of Control) together. I knew her well then and have admired her through the years. She is Barbara Ballard, the wife of Elder M. Russell Ballard, who is one of the Twelve Apostles.

Another wonderful high school girl who sang one of the leads in our school operetta, and who was always vivacious, outgoing, sweet, and bright, was also active in the Church. She married Bob Zarboch, with whom I played football. He has been a bishop and served in many high places in the Church. She has sung in the Tabernacle Choir for years. Her talented voice has contributed to every ward in which she has lived. She has sung hundreds and hundreds of times, sharing her voice in acts of service. Her future was as predictable as Bob's, who has always been honorable and an extremely hard worker.

There was another girl in my school who had a reputation which was not quite as desirable. The boys in school talked about her loose morals. Although she was a beautiful young woman, she used her "sex appeal" for popularity. She married early and divorced soon. She has been through several marriages. Her features are now coarse and rough.

Abraham Lincoln stated that a man over forty is responsible for his own face. A woman is responsible for her beauty also. This woman had little understanding of fidelity and faithfulness. She always had a "roving eye" where men were concerned. Her life is sad and broken. The hard, uncontrolled life of indulgence and compromise has left its mark. The future for this woman is as bleak as her present. She has no posterity to bring her joy, only several shattered marriages with accompanying hurt and heartache. Unless she changes—repents and finds Christ in her life—she will live her life out as a coarse, lonely, pitiful woman. It need not have been this way. All it would have taken on her part was to have become a living commitment to moral principles.

The first Court of Honor I ever attended as a Scout was the most memorable. Jim Rasband received his Life Scout rank. I will never forget the feelings of admiration and respect that I felt for him at that time. It gave me a goal to become a Life Scout. Later Jim received his Eagle Scout Award. I also made a goal to become an Eagle. Over the years I have caught only small snatches of information about Jim Rasband, but his future was predictable. He chose the higher road, the more noble walk through life. His influence has reached out to hundreds and thousands, directly and indirectly.

In contrast, one of the most crude human beings I ever met was in high school with us. His every sentence contained obscenities, filthy language, blasphemous statements, and profanity. He waded in mental sewage all through high school. He always told dirty stories and boasted about his self-abuse, the girls he conquered, and stealing experiences. He was as uncouth as any man, old or young, that I have ever met. He never achieved anything in high school. About all he ever did was attend class and frustrate the class work. I do not think he even knew how to have clean, honest fun. He smoked and drank and fooled around with drugs. He had absolutely abandoned a life of discipline. One could almost have predicted what would become of him—barring repentance. Now he is old before his time, wrinkled, and without energy. There is a spirit of evil about him, and little children shy away from him. Imagine what a difference it might have made if the Church and Scouting had been important to him.

I believe that hiking in beautiful wilderness areas; camping on a high, lush meadow; climbing craggy cliffs; swimming in pure mountain lakes and streams; fishing on a quiet river bank; watching the eagles and hawks soar through high skies; feeling refreshing rain fall on an upturned face; kneeling in prayer in a quiet pine grove—such activities could have redirected his life. But he chose otherwise. He became addicted to the tormentings of the flesh and now has been shackled head and foot by Satan, who smirks and laughs. Wickedness never, worlds without end, will bring happiness, only sorrow and misery.

I was raised in Richards Ward in the Sugar House Stake. We had a lot of youth in the ward. I believe about thirteen couples married within the ward. We were all active and were deeply involved in all the activities of the Church.

One night during a bishop's discussion we were not listening; we were fooling around instead. The bishop stopped his talk and in a firm voice said to us: "You need to get serious. One day some of you will be bishops, some stake presidents, and one of you may well be a General Authority." All the girls in the group hooted to think any one of the fellows would ever be a General Authority. The bishop then turned to the girls and said, "You laugh at that but one of you may be married to him."

It is interesting that I was in the group that night and that one of the girls who laughed the hardest was Merlene Miner. Later she became my wife. It was not necessarily predictable that one of the group would be a General Authority, but it was highly predictable that some would be bishops, some in stake presidencies, some mission presidents, general board members, Relief Society, Primary, and Young Women presidents. Young men and women from that group have served in every call mentioned above. We had a great time as ward members, our dances were fun, and we did not pair off until some time later. Preparation with the help of good leaders moved us toward our callings.

You can see into the future and know what is going to happen. The future can be predicted and, of course, prophesied.

Rebellion is dangerous and leads only to misery and unhappiness. Obedience is doing things God's way because it is the best way and will bring us the least personal problems. There are benefits that come from living the gospel of Jesus Christ and keeping his commandments. They include a sweet, spiritual, fulfilled mission, and being dressed in white and kneeling at an altar in the temple across from the man or woman you adore. They include health and happiness, opportunities to serve, to be fulfilled, to live within your income, to be free from the bondage of debt, the burden of sin, and strength to endure the trials of life.

Each of us after some intense thinking can see into the future and make certain predictions with relative accuracy. Why not take time now to meditate and determine where your present course will lead if you continue as at present? If it appears that it will not bring contentment, peace, service, purity, love, fidelity, and spiritual success, then rechart your course. Pray faithfully daily, read the scriptures daily, make decisions of certain things you will and will not do. Then, stay on course and God's light will bring you to a safe harbor of all you prize and hold dear.

CHAPTER NINETEEN

Think, Believe, Dream, Dare

The story is told of a boy who wanted to meet the wisest man in the world. He searched long and far and finally met him. The boy wanted to know what advice this wisest of all men would give him. His advice was: Think, believe, dream, dare.

Thinking takes energy. It is a discipline. Some have referred to it as headwork or brainwork, and both are accurate. Thinking is work. Thinking has many faces, such as pondering, musing, considering, reasoning, deliberating, cogitating, dreaming, and studying.

There is positive and negative thinking. Positive thinking is exciting, creative, and fulfilling. It builds and brings about action or results. It can be stimulating, as it is when we solve a difficult problem. It lifts and motivates us to do better. It leads toward a habit that will prove to be a benefit all of our lives.

Negative thinking involves useless worry, jealousy, letting the mind wander, thinking about pornography, self-depreciation, working up lies, hating, and such things. Negative thinking is destructive to self and our relationships with others, and it brings sadness, sickness, and possible mental illness. It also can become habit-forming and consumes inordinate amounts of energy and time, and generally accomplishes nothing. Some educators claim that the mind rests only a few moments a day. One thing is certain; we all know how active it can be.

In the story you were told at the beginning of this chapter, the wisest man said, "Think." Consider this poem by Rudyard Kipling entitled "If." I have committed it to memory. When you memorize something, you always have it with you, and you can draw on it at any moment. It becomes part of you. Here is a poem by a man who has given a great deal of thought about what constitutes a man or a woman.

If

If you can keep your head when all about you
Are losing theirs and blaming it on you;
If you can trust yourself when all men doubt you,
But make allowance for their doubting too;
If you can wait and not be tired by waiting,
Or, being lied about, don't deal in lies,
Or, being hated, don't give way to hating,
And yet don't look too good, nor talk too wise;

If you can dream—and not make dreams your master;
If you can think—and not make thoughts your aim;
If you can meet with triumph and disaster
And treat those two imposters just the same;
If you can bear to hear the truth you've spoken
Twisted by knaves to make a trap for fools,
Or watch the things you gave your life to broken,
And stoop and build 'em up with worn-out tools;

If you can make one heap of all your winnings
And risk it on one turn of pitch-and-toss,
And lose, and start again at your beginnings
And never breathe a word about your loss;
If you can force your heart and nerve and sinew
To serve your turn long after they are gone,
And so hold on when there is nothing in you
Except the Will which says to them: "Hold on";

If you can talk with crowds and keep your virtue,
Or walk with kings—nor lose the common touch;
If neither foes nor loving friends can hurt you;
If all men count with you, but none too much;
If you can fill the unforgiving minute
With sixty seconds' worth of distance run—
Yours is the Earth and everything that's in it,
and—which is more—you'll be a Man, my son!

Remember he said, "If you can dream—and not make dreams your master;/If you can think—and not make thoughts your aim." He is, I think, saying to us that we should use thoughts in a productive way to assist us in achieving our goals. Direct our thinking; ponder, study, and pray about the purpose behind our thoughts. I recently spoke at a Brigham Young University devotional. It took a great deal of thought to determine a subject that would be of value. I decided to speak about the counsel the prophet would give if he were there. This was an intense experience. I read and pondered the words of the prophet, then I considered what he had said in the past, and eventually put it all on paper.

You should involve deep thinking about your conduct. Be prepared for the unexpected, and I promise you that even then you will be surprised many times. Think about what you will do when confronted with a staggering temptation.

A young man, clean and pure, left his home one evening with his friends. He loved the Lord and he loved the Church. He was active and had no vices. His friends picked him up and took him out to drag Main Street. They met a carload of girls and paired off. The girl he paired off with had been around, was not a member of the Church, and had a different set of values. In just a moment his virtue was lost; everything he had prized and held dear was shattered. A total life of doing the good and right things bruised by an act of fornication. He went directly to his bishop as heartbroken as any young man I have witnessed. My friends, ahead of time think of what you will do when served with various temptations. Think of the consequences to you, the Church, your family, your future. Take time to think of your values and how important they are to you.

Samuel Smiles stated, "It is the mind that sees as well as the eye" (Smiles, *Happy Homes*, p. 244). Solomon said, "The wise man's eyes are in his head, but the fool walketh in darkness" (Ecclesiastes 2:14).

The suspension bridge was invented because Captain Brown observed a tiny spider's web as he walked through his garden. It set his mind to thinking. It was the sight of seaweed floating past his ship that enabled Columbus to quell the mutiny which arose amongst his sailors. (Smiles, *Happy Homes*, p. 246.)

Samuel Smiles also stated:

> Sedulous attention and painstaking industry always mark the true worker. The greatest men are not those who "despise the day of small things," but those who improve them the most carefully. Michael Angelo was one day explaining to a visitor to his studio what he had been doing at a statue since his previous visit. "I have retouched this part—polished that—softened this feature—brought out that muscle—given some expression to this lip, and more energy to that limb." "But these are trifles," remarked the visitor. "It may be so," replied the sculptor, "but recollect that trifles make perfection, and perfection is no trifle."

"Believe," said the wise man. This can be applied to many things. Believe in God and have confidence in the faith of your parents. Believe in yourself that you are a child of the Eternal Father. The Lord wants you to be successful. He said, "Be ye therefore perfect, even as your Father which is in heaven is perfect" (Matthew 5:48).

We had a missionary in the field who was one of the finest missionaries I have ever known. He had all the discussions memorized, word perfect, soon after arriving in the mission. He was confident, loved people, and had a great heart for the work. He was a believer.

I learned from him as he left the mission (having served as a training senior companion, a district leader, a zone leader, a presiding zone leader, and an assistant to the president) that his life had been hard. The members of his family were all active in the Church. One night when his father, who was in a presiding role in a Church assignment, returned home, his wife was gone. They had a large family. She had left a note that she was leaving and not to try to find her. She had abandoned a husband and several children, and they did not hear from her again.

This Elder said that he went to school (he was in about the ninth grade) but he longed and grieved for his mother. He wondered how she could just up and leave without seemingly any attachment. He began to do very poorly in school. He could not sleep at night. He died inside and lost all desire to live. His noble father did what he could but it did not help much. The family deteriorated without the mother in the home. His grieving was followed by anger and then resentment toward his mother. Finally he began to believe in himself again. He succeeded in school and athletics. He became a well adjusted person and had found the Lord during this agonizing ordeal. Faith and belief replaced sorrow and sadness. He went on to become a great missionary.

Helen Keller's teacher believed that Helen could learn, and she bent every talent, skill, and all her being to break through the seemingly impenetrable curtain to her mind. She finally succeeded because she believed she could do it.

The Prophet Joseph, as a boy, believed what he read in the Bible. Not only did he believe but it seemed to set his soul on fire. What would happen if all of us would believe with that same intensity Joseph had. He literally believed, "If any of you lack wisdom, let him ask of God, that giveth to all men liberally, and upbraideth not; and it shall be given him" (James 1:5). My, what a marvelous church this would be if we all had such strong belief. As a result of his belief and faith, he bore a testimony that I have memorized, because when I read it I believed it was true. Yes, I know it was true.

> However, it was nevertheless a fact that I had beheld a vision. I have thought since, that I felt much like Paul, when he made his defense before King Agrippa, and related the account of the vision he had when he saw a light, and heard a voice; but still there were but few who believed him; some said he was dishonest, others said he was mad; and he was ridiculed and reviled. But all this did not destroy the reality of his vision. He had seen a vision, he knew he had, and all the persecution under heaven could not make it otherwise; and though they should persecute him unto death, yet he knew, and would know to his latest breath, that he had both seen a

light and heard a voice speaking unto him, and all the world could not make him think or believe otherwise.

So it was with me. I had actually seen a light, and in the midst of that light I saw two Personages, and they did in reality speak to me; and though I was hated and persecuted for saying that I had seen a vision, yet it was true; and while they were persecuting me, reviling me, and speaking all manner of evil against me falsely for so saying, I was led to say in my heart: Why persecute me for telling the truth? I have actually seen a vision; and who am I that I can withstand God, or why does the world think to make me deny what I have actually seen? For I had seen a vision; I knew it, and I knew that God knew it, and I could not deny it, neither dared I do it; at least I knew that by so doing I would offend God, and come under condemnation. (Joseph Smith—History 1:24–25.)

It is a great blessing to have a believing heart. "Dream"—for dreams truly can come to pass. The prophets of God have always been men of vision. "Behind every great achievement is a dreamer of great dreams" (Greenleaf, *Servant Leadership* [Ramsey, New Jersey: Paulist Press, 1977]).

Abraham Lincoln had a dream that one day every citizen of this United States of America would be free. President Spencer W. Kimball had a dream that one day all worthy male members would hold the priesthood. He had a dream of temples across the land. He dreamed of a force of missionaries that startled the non-dreamers. He had a dream about the Lamanites and became a protecting father and prophet to them.

J. Willard Marriott, Sr., had a dream that grew from an A&W root beer stand to a corporation that staggers the imagination. Lord Baden-Powell dreamed that boys could become Scouts, and his dream has penetrated every continent. Every Olympic athlete has had a dream that he or she would participate in this world-wide competition. Many dreamed of gold medals.

Dreaming with a purpose is not for the lazy. Dreaming requires performance to make the dream a reality. President Spencer W. Kimball said, "Make no small plans; they have no magic to stir men's souls." Thank the Lord for men and women of vision—those who dream dreams, who make no small plans.

Elisha the prophet could see beyond the veil. In this marvelous account from 2 Kings, we read:

And it was so, when Elisha the man of God had heard that the king of Israel had rent his clothes, that he sent to the king, saying, Wherefore hast thou rent thy clothes? let him come now to me, and he shall know that there is a prophet in Israel.

So Naaman came with his horses and with his chariot, and stood at the door of the house of Elisha.

And Elisha sent a messenger unto him, saying, Go and wash in Jordan seven times, and thy flesh shall come again to thee, and thou shalt be clean.

But Naaman was wroth, and went away, and said, Behold, I thought, He will surely come out to me, and stand, and call on the name of the Lord his God, and strike his hand over the place, and recover the leper.

Are not Abana and Pharpar, rivers of Damascus, better than all the waters of Israel: may I not wash in them, and be clean? So he turned and went away in a rage.

And his servants came near, and spake unto him, and said, My father, if the prophet had bid thee do some great thing, wouldest thou not have done it? how much rather then, when he saith to thee, Wash, and be clean?

Then went he down, and dipped himself seven times in Jordan, according to the saying of the man of God: and his flesh came again like unto the flesh of a little child, and he was clean.

And he returned to the man of God, he and all his company, and came, and stood before him: and he said, Behold, now I know that there is no God in all the earth, but in Israel: now therefore, I pray thee, take a blessing of thy servant.

But he said, As the Lord liveth, before whom I stand, I will receive none. And he urged him to take it; but he refused.

And Naaman said, Shall there not then, I pray thee, be given to thy servant two mules' burden of earth? for thy servant will hence-forth offer neither burnt offering nor sacrifice unto other gods, but unto the Lord. (2 Kings 5:8–17.)

Visions and dreams must not be confused with laziness and daydreaming, without any control over the mind. Dreamers are creative.

Dare means *to do*. This must be used wisely, not foolishly. To dare means to venture forth. William James, the great psychologist, said:

Man alone, of all the creatures of earth, can change his own pattern. Man alone is architect of his destiny. The greatest revolution in our generation is the discovery that human beings, by changing the inner attitudes of their minds, can change the outer aspects of their lives. (As quoted in a periodical from the Executive Dynamics Foundation, Glendale, California.)

In a commencement speech delivered by Harvey C. Jacobs, editor of the *Indianapolis News* to the graduates of Franklin College in Indiana he said:

> In a Japanese novel of several years ago the main character, wandering in a strange village, becomes trapped at the bottom of a sand pit. Food and water are lowered to him, but no ladder. He wants out, desperately. He begs his captors to let him go. He tries to bargain with them, but nothing works. Months pass. The begging, the scheming become a way of life.
>
> After a long time he is granted what he wants, what he has been striving for with all his will, day and night: the freedom to come out of his pit and go on his way, in complete freedom. Suddenly, he is afraid. He is alarmed by the prospect of facing the world without protection. He could get lost, he thinks. In his little pit he was at least sheltered from unknown harm.
>
> And now he understand that freedom is not a reward, but a terrible risk. ("You *Can* Take It with You: Freedom—A Terrible Risk," in *Vital Speeches of the Day*, vol. 50, no. 19 [Southold, New York: City News Publishing Co., 1974], p. 603.)

To dare also implies risk. I recall the essence of a statement by Helmut Schmidt, the Chancellor of West Germany. Although it has a ring of amusement, there is also a ring of truth. He said that "in the very beginning of any project there was great enthusiasm, followed by doubt, then panic, then search for the guilty party, punishing of the innocent and rewarding of the uninvolved."

In your lifetime you will see this little bit of philosophy enacted over and over again. Those who dare will feel the bite. It takes courage to dare. Those who have dared have walked on the moon as well as gone to the North and South poles. They have walked on the ocean floors and stood on Mount Everest. They have started organizations, companies, and corporations which have employed thousands of workers.

The company for which I worked for many years was known as Albertson's, Inc. It was started years back. Joe Albertson worked for a large chain. As a young man he had ascended the corporate ladder to a district manager level. He felt to strike out on his own, which he did in Boise, Idaho. He bought a small store and opened for business. The company for which he had previously worked decided to put him out of business. They cut the prices in the store nearest to him. They sold below cost and attempted to bankrupt this young entrepreneur. At the end of the first year of operation Joe Albertson had generated only two thousand dollars profit, having worked the whole year from fifteen to twenty hours a day, but he was still in business.

The neighboring store restored their operation to normal and thus began a story of a dreamer who dared. Now Albertson's sales are in the billions, and tens of thousands of people find employment in his stores. He dared to try.

Those who dare are doers. I have watched missionaries over the years and have noted that there are those who dare to be challenging and testifying missionaries, and they reap great success.

Devin Durrant dared to interrupt his college basketball career and go on a mission, and he came back to achieve national All-American status and to become one of the highest point scorers in the nation.

There are those who dare to trust in the Lord and who dare to keep his commandments. There are those who dare to say no to evil and corruption and who maintain their integrity. There are those who dare to do anything the Lord suggests they do. They are not ashamed—they simply know that none of us can ever get into the Lord's debt.

Dare to do right for all that is in you.

According to the story, the boy was told by the "wisest man" in the world: *Think, believe, dream, dare.* A great message for our generation.

CHAPTER TWENTY

Ambassadors of Truth

During a mission tour at a zone conference, a young black man was asked to bear his testimony. I wrote down the following as he talked: "I learned good from other people. I realized the missionaries were doing the work of Christ. They had the gospel and they brought it to me. Satan tried to get me to not listen to the missionaries. He tried to involve me in the 'colors' game. I wondered why the confrontation with Satan. Then I realized I was at the door of the true church and Satan did not want me to enter. This church has shown me the greatest love I have ever known. Once I had accepted the gospel, I wanted to let the whole world know about it. I wanted it for everyone in the neighborhood, for all my friends, but they did not want it. My heart ached and I was sad for them. Now I feel like a poor beggar that was given a field of diamonds." What this young man stated was not far from the Savior's parable of a pearl of great price.

This young man had bought a new pair of corduroys just to be dressed appropriately for the zone conference. He had taken off the tag, but had left the thread that fastened the tag on. He was poor but had a sense of being appropriately groomed to talk to the missionaries.

Another black woman said that she worked at a hospital as a nurse from eleven at night until seven in the morning. She had three teenage children and no husband. The music in their home was hard rock and it caused contention. The home was not clean. Every morning after work she picked up a six-pack of beer to drink during the day. She smoked and she drank coffee.

One morning while she was sleeping, the missionaries came. She did not want to answer the door but something inside her urged her to do it. She invited the missionaries in and listened to the first discussion. Over the next few weeks they returned and taught her all the discussions. Then this good woman said: "My three teenage children and I were baptized into the Church. I still work all night as a nurse, but I don't drink anymore. I do not smoke. I do not drink coffee. Our family goes to church together. We have family prayer and hold family home evening. My house is clean and the hard rock music is gone. I love the Church."

Another woman, a mother of nine children, bore her testimony in these words: "Over the many months I thought I had seen all the LDS missionaries in my home. We have had seventeen Elders and two Sisters." She also worked all night. She said: "For many years I had prayed and I had searched for this day. What would be greater than to serve the Lord Jesus Christ? I was baptized a Baptist at age twelve and my mother was a really good Christian. However, I felt what I was hearing my minister teach was not true. I then joined the Presbyterian church and could not find truth. Then in the Jehovah Witnesses church, I found only part of the truth. When I heard the Joseph Smith story, I knew it was true. I had prayed to the Lord to show me the true church for five years. I had stopped attending my church and waited for the Lord to teach me the truth. A year later two missionaries came to my home. I felt, while they were teaching me, as though a blade of fire was in my soul. What a blessing it is to know that God is our Father, that Jesus Christ is his son.

"One night during the time the missionaries were teaching me, I was awakened at 3:00 A.M. Satan visited me. I heard footsteps. He moved up to the side of the bed and I felt pressure binding my head. I sat up in bed and began to pray and the darkness left and a sweet voice said, 'You must be baptized into the Church of Jesus Christ.' ''

Some of you may have heard me bear my testimony that this church is true, that we are not playing games. There is a prophet at the head who receives revelation and direction. We do have twelve special witnesses—the Quorum of the Twelve Apostles—who testify of the living Christ.

The previous experiences are similar to the ones you can have in the mission field. The purpose of this chapter is to assist you in preparing to become an ambassador of the Lord.

President Spencer W. Kimball stated that every worthy young man is expected to serve on a mission. If a young man is not worthy, he should become worthy. In my understanding of the above statement, no one is exempt. Many young women will serve missions. If a young lady has a desire to serve a mission, she should counsel with her bishop and make the necessary preparations. And of course we also have our mature Saints who are so effective and bring such a strength to missionary work.

Following is a list of success principles which, if followed, will help you become a more productive, successful, fulfilled missionary. They are not in order of importance but rather are basically in order of your preparation:

1. *Make a commitment* that when you enter the mission field you will live every mission rule. This means 100 percent of them. Do not attempt to be selective; live them all. Sometimes those that seem to be lesser rules are the ones that refine and polish us to the point where we really obtain blessings from heaven.

2. *Read the Joseph Smith story,* or the account in Joseph Smith—History in the Pearl of Great Price, every week. This will allow the Holy Ghost continually to reaffirm the fact that Joseph was a prophet. President Ezra Taft Benson has given this as counsel to all missionaries.

3. *Read the little white Missionary Handbook* every week. Carry it with you at all times. Let it become your "Liahona." Use it as a guide.

4. *Dress for success.* Be certain that your dress and grooming reflect the dignity of your call as an ambassador of the Lord Jesus

Christ. How we dress has an effect on our conduct. Everyone in the Church seems to pay particular attention to missionaries' grooming and conduct. Once they have confidence in the missionaries, they will introduce them to their nonmember friends.

5. *Learn proper prayer.* The Spirit is very sensitive. It is easily offended. The wrong thought, an unkind act, uncouthness, loud and obnoxious laughter, light-mindedness, and similar behavior all cause a spiritual withdrawal. When you think about having the companionship of the Holy Ghost, consider what your conduct should be. The Holy Ghost is the third member of the Godhead. You must consider what your conduct would be if the Savior walked with you daily. So it is with the Holy Ghost. If you desire to have the Spirit with you, to have your prayers be effective, you must avoid those thoughts and actions that cause it to withdraw.

We need the Holy Ghost so we will know the things for which we should pray. Prayer does not always require great amounts of time. There may be occasions, however, when it will. For the most part we need to make our prayers an earnest, thoughtful, spiritual experience with a Father who loves us and responds to our righteous desires.

Consider your relationship with Heavenly Father in the way you might consider an interview with your earthly father. You would want to tell him the things that trouble your heart. You would listen and regard his counsel. You would surely consider his direction, for you know his interests would be in your behalf.

Talk with God. Do it even when it is most difficult. He is a loving parent who regards you as his offspring. He will never abandon you. Counsel with him and listen carefully during your prayers and throughout the day. Answers will come. The still, small voice will guide you, but remember it is a still, *small* voice.

6. *Study the scriptures.* One of the most thrilling experiences a young person can have is a discovery of the scriptures. Once during my very young years—I was perhaps nine—I earned a quarter. Costs were quite different then. You might find it hard to believe, but at Woolworth's I was able to buy with my quarter a Holy Bible with a thin cardboard cover. I carried it home in the sack, and when I arrived home I took it out of the sack and held it to my bosom. I felt a thrill of ownership and a spiritual witness

that the Bible contained truth that I would need to know. I read a little from it at that time and did not understand much. Nonetheless, I always treasured it.

My mother recently passed away. As the family sorted through her things after the funeral, they came across this old Bible that I had bought forty-five years ago. As I picked it up, I had the same sensations of sweetness go through my being, and I knew again that it contained truth.

Imagine the influence of the scriptures in my life over the years. I have read and reread the Book of Mormon, the Doctrine and Covenants, and the Pearl of Great Price. All of these scriptures bear witness of the truths contained in the Bible. Would to God that words could somehow express the deep, abiding love and affection that I have for the scriptures!

Decide to read the scriptures each day. If it is difficult in the morning, read in the evening, or right after school. Do not set a goal of an hour or even a half hour in the beginning. Start with reading a chapter or two. Do not be concerned if you do not comprehend all that you read. You will be acquainting yourself with the language of the prophets. There will come a measure of understanding and it will increase. Then you will desire to read more and more of the sacred words of the prophets. The important thing is to start and to continue until a habit is formed.

7. *Have the spiritual strength and maturity to love the standards of the Church* even if you have to "buck the norm." The term *norm* is an abbreviation of *normative behavior* or a description of what most people do. For example, a norm in a ward might be for every deacon, teacher, and priest to wear a dress shirt and tie and possibly a suit or sportcoat while officiating in the sacrament service. This is a positive norm that should be encouraged. A negative norm would be if the members of the Aaronic Priesthood officiated in inappropriate shirts, without ties or suits, and then after the sacrament they quickly exited the chapel and went out into the foyer and made light of sacred things.

We realize it may be difficult to "buck" or go against a powerful negative norm, but hundreds and thousands have done it with positive results. There is a great army of youth who make positive contributions. They will lead out in church activities and their peers will recognize the self-discipline they have. They will become leaders at school and in other activities. All of us know the young men and women who are true to their standards, and no matter whether people like them or not, they are always respected. I would a thousand times rather be respected than liked if I had to be one or the other. Thank goodness for those who are respected, and generally liked, because their conduct is not offensive to other youth of substance.

The standards of the Church are known by members and non-members. The Word of Wisdom is a towering, inspired revelation for healthful living. Chastity represents an attitude of purity of mind and body. The chaste or virtuous individual truly is a person who has control of life. There are consequences that come to those who are not chaste. There are the well-known venereal diseases that bring sorrow, embarrassment, sickness, and ill health. There are other consequences that are not as well known, but which can result in AIDS, mental illness, and similar devastating and possibly life-threatening conditions.

The standards of the Church assist us in maintaining a level of conduct that will keep us from the quicksand of major transgression. Some of these standards include not dating until you are sixteen, not dating outside of the Church membership, and not dating faithless members of the Church. Others include appropriate music, honesty, avoiding pornography and drugs, and associating with close personal friends who have equally high standards.

The positive side of upholding the standards of the Church is that they bring happiness, excitement, joy, pleasure, self-confidence, self-esteem, and a sense of self-worth. Church standards are provided so that all of us, young and old, might have guidelines for living that are inspired and revealed by God through his holy prophets for our benefit. We are truly free when we keep the commandments.

Youth who have been involved in major transgressions must be cleared by a General Authority before they are permitted to be called on missions. Those who have kept themselves pure, who have lived the standards, avoid these kinds of problems.

8. *Take advantage of your schooling.* The ability to study, concentrate, and train your mind is the objective of schooling. How foolish we are if we waste precious hours that would benefit us all our lives. Education teaches us how to apply the knowledge and principles we learn.

Those who have disciplined themselves to study and who have made a conscious effort to earn good grades in school have an advantage in the mission field. They have a developed skill that is sharp and works to their good.

Pray about what classes you should take. Take all the English, language, or communication classes you can. These will benefit you all your life. Life is a process of communicating with others. How well we do it determines how successful we will be not only on our missions but also and especially throughout life. Also take math classes. They are an exact science and will prove important throughout your life. We also mention languages. The First Presidency has counseled the youth to take several years of a language.

You can do well in school with proper application and attention. There will still be plenty of time to join in all the activities and fun. Sometime just a little extra effort in school brings about a very healthy improvement in your grade point average.

This chapter is not all-inclusive. Every other chapter has information that will assist you in becoming a faithful ambassador of Christ. The experiences mentioned at the beginning of this chapter will be paralleled by your own mission experiences. They bring greater joy than you would ever suppose. Imagine the feelings of the missionaries who had taught each of these people. There were tears shed and hearts filled to overflowing.

Do not leave your missionary preparation until the day you are formally called to be an ambassador of truth. Begin now. Prepare now. You will be blessed beyond measure.

CHAPTER TWENTY-ONE

A Generation of Leaders

My beloved young men of the Aaronic Priesthood and young women. We live in a great day in the history of the world. We live in the dispensation of the fulness of times. What a wonderful blessing to be young at this time. I would like to take a moment to give you a vision of who you are and what marvelous things you will do.

You are marvelous young women, endowed with talents, skills, and abilities to exceed any other generation. You will stand as a giant bulwark of righteousness in modern Israel. You will stand on pedestals with your husband in his high priesthood callings. You will mother the great leaders who will rule this kingdom and carry it into the millennium. You will be the pure example of great womanhood—chaste, clean, and virtuous—with absolute faith in Christ.

You young men are an army of Aaronic Priesthood bearers—the largest army of young men ever assembled. Within your ranks are future Apostles and prophets, stake and mission presidents, Regional Representatives, bishops, and the greatest missionaries of all time.

The Lord said, "But first let my army become very great, and let it be sanctified before me, that it may become fair as the sun, and clear as the moon, and that her banners may be terrible unto all nations; that the kingdoms of this world may be constrained to acknowledge that the kingdom of Zion is in very deed the kingdom of our God and his Christ; therefore, let us become subject unto her laws." (D&C 105:31–32.)

To be sanctified means to become pure and holy. You will dream dreams and see visions. Angels will attend you. You will gather strength and wisdom from all other generations, and with great power you will move forth to more fully establish the kingdom of God. You will lift a standard that shall shine as a celestial beacon during the darkest hours in the history of man. In a day when there is great compromise, you will be true. In a day when idleness and laziness is common, you will labor with uncommon energy. When minds are shriveling from lack of use, yours will be expanding with intelligence and enlightenment from God. Great hosts will sink in the degradation of homosexuality, fornication, and pornography, but you will shine as fair as the sun. In a time when men are turning from God and satisfying their own greedy indulgences to "eat, drink, and be merry," you will march under the white banners of purity in a modern crusade for Christ that will startle the world.

Oh, my beloved young friends, however insecure you feel, no matter how few talents you may feel you have, no matter how insignificant you may be told you are, do not believe it. Young men, you are sons of God, royal priesthood bearers. Every one of you is destined to lead.

Vice President Bush shared an inspiring story at the national meetings of the Boy Scouts of America.

> Way back in 401 B.C., a young Persian prince named Cyrus hired an army of 10,000 Greek soldiers to help him take the Persian throne away from his brother. Cyrus and his Greek companions marched 1500 miles overland from the western edge of Turkey, through the deserts of Syria, and onto the plains of Iraq, where they met the Persian king. They met the Persian king and the army near what is now Bagdad. The Greeks won the battle, but they lost the war when Cyrus was killed in the day's action, and that left the Greeks and

their army in a terrible fix. They no longer had any cause to proceed
further; they couldn't retreat eastward, for no food remained on the
land, and to the north, mountains, which we know today as the wilds
of Cartistan and the highlands of Georgia and Armenia, were all
inhabited by savage mountain tribes. And to make things worse, the
Greek commanding general and his entire staff of officers had gone
to a conference with the Persians under safe conduct, and they had
been assassinated. And that seemed to leave absolutely no alternative to the Greeks but to surrender and throw themselves on the
mercy of the Persians. Some of you will remember this. One of the
Greeks, a private in the ranks named Xenophon, had a different idea,
and he voiced it to his Greek comrades: "Notice that our enemies
lacked the courage to fight us until they seized our general. They
think that we are defeated because our officers are dead, but we'll
show them that they turned us all into generals. Instead of one
general, they'll have 10,000 generals against them." The Greeks'
spirits rallied and they resolved to fight their way through the mountains. Xenophon turned out to be a brilliant strategist and his army
of 10,000 generals did reach safety, 2500 miles and four months later.
Perhaps the most celebrated march of that time, celebrated escape, if
you will, in western history. (From an unpublished address given at
the 75th Anniversary Dinner of the Boy Scouts of America, February
7, 1985.)

Through righteous membership in this kingdom, you will be
turned into hundreds of thousands of generals and the most
blessed mothers to walk the earth.

Another great general, Antigonus, had never lost a battle. One
time he engaged an enemy that greatly outnumbered them. He
called his captains together and they worked out a particular
strategy to assault the enemy and win the battle. General
Antigonus was to give the signal after all the men had been
briefed by their captains. The signal was given, but no one
attacked. In fact, they were about to retreat ingloriously. General
Antigonus called his captains together to see why the men had
not attacked on the given signal. The captains replied that the
men would not attack, because they were outnumbered severely.
Not only would they not attack but they were also about to
retreat. General Antigonus took a few steps and looked out over
the battlefield. Then he turned back to his captains, and with a
jaw set in steel and eyes that penetrated every captain, he said,

"How many do you count me for?" That spirit thrilled the captains and it set the hearts of the soldiers aflame. They attacked and won a great victory.

How many do you count a prophet of God for? How many do you count an Apostle, a mission president, your stake president, or bishop, for? How many do you count your father for? How many do you count your mother for?

Some of the youth of this generation will achieve victories as monumental as David did over Goliath. It is thrilling to read how David "hasted, and ran toward the army to meet the Philistine" (1 Samuel 17:48).

We read of Daniel, who was the interpreter of King Nebuchadnezzar's dream, and who was rejected by the governors and princes who conspired against him. But Daniel was preferred above the presidents and the princes "because an *excellent spirit* was in him; and the king thought to set him over the whole realm" (Daniel 6:3; italics added).

Shadrach, Meshach, and Abed-nego were taken before King Nebuchadnezzar, who commanded them to fall down and worship the golden image he had created. Those who would not worship the golden image were cast into the burning, fiery furnace. The king himself addressed these wonderful Hebrew princes: "Is it true, O Shadrach, Meshach, and Abed-nego, do not ye serve my gods, nor worship the golden image which I have set up? Now if ye be ready that at what time ye hear the sound of the cornet, flute, harp, sackbut, psaltery, and dulcimer, and all kinds of musick, ye fall down and worship the image which I have made; well: but if ye worship not, ye shall be cast the same hour into the midst of a burning fiery furnace; and who is that God that shall deliver you out of my hands?" (Daniel 3:14–15.)

This was no small contest between principles and integrity, loyalty and faith in Christ. Their answer rings with clarity down through the centuries. What courage, what faith! Shadrach, Meshach, and Abed-nego answered and said to the king: "O Nebuchadnezzar, we are not careful to answer thee in this matter. If it be so, our God whom we serve is able to deliver us from the burning fiery furnace, and he will deliver us out of thine hand, O king. But if not, be it known unto thee, O king, that we will not serve thy gods, nor worship the golden image which thou hast set up." (Daniel 3:16–18.)

Young Mormon, at the age of ten, was approached by Ammaron, who had "hid up the records." Ammaron said to him, "I perceive that thou art a sober child, and art quick to observe." Then he gave Mormon a charge that when he was about twenty-four years old he was to "go to the land Antum, unto a hill which shall be called Shim; and there have I deposited unto the Lord all the sacred engravings concerning this people." (Mormon 1:2–3.) My young friends, you do not have to wait until you have sixty years of experience. Learn in thy youth. Prepare now. Enlist in this great work. There is much for you to do.

At the age of sixteen, Mormon became the general over all the Nephite armies, and he remained a general throughout his life. He still was their general at age seventy-four. Near the end of his life, he gave his son Moroni an account of the wickedness and degradation of the army which he led, and then said: "And now, my son, I dwell no longer upon this horrible scene. Behold, thou knowest the wickedness of this people; thou knowest that they are without principle, and past feeling; and their wickedness doth exceed that of the Lamanites. Behold, my son, I cannot recommend them unto God lest he should smite me." (Moroni 9:20–21.)

But listen to the supreme compliment and the profound respect and tender feelings he had for his son: "But behold, my son, I recommend thee unto God, and I trust in Christ that thou wilt be saved; and I pray unto God that he will spare thy life, to witness the return of his people unto him, or their utter destruction; for I know that they must perish except they repent and return unto him" (Moroni 9:22).

Consider the role of Mary the mother of our Lord. Has ever a handmaiden of the Lord been more blessed? Imagine what it would be to carry the very Son of God in your womb. Think of the feeling that filled her breast when Jesus was born.

Who trained and nurtured David, Daniel, Shadrach, Meshach, Abed-nego, Mormon, and Moroni? Who but wonderful mothers who made their contribution to the kingdom through their sons and daughters? It was the women who stood by, prayed for, and shared in their husbands' tasks. Men and women have separate and distinct roles in the eternal scheme of things, but each are equally important.

Joseph F. Smith left his widowed mother and sailed alone to Hawaii, where he filled his first mission at the age of fifteen. As a priest with a missionary companion, Wilford Woodruff walked for miles in a swamp. When young Wilford hurt his knee and couldn't go on, his companion left him in the swamp and said he was returning to his home in Kirtland. Wilford Woodruff knelt in the swamp and pleaded with the Lord. A healing blessing came to his leg and he journeyed many miles on to continue his ministry.

The young friends of Tommy Monson often chided him and called him ''bishop'' while he was only a deacon or teacher. One day his mother heard them jesting, calling him a ''bishop.'' She said to them, ''That's all right, boys, one day he will be a bishop'' —which he was at twenty-two, a short time after his marriage. He was in a stake presidency at twenty-seven, a mission president at twenty-nine, and an Apostle at age thirty-four.

Years ago I remember Bishop Carl Buehner of the Presiding Bishopric sharing a story of a deacons quorum president in Idaho who walked several miles through knee-deep snow so he could get out to the road to catch a ride to the Saturday night stake conference leadership meeting he was invited to attend. That story had a real influence on my life.

As a teachers quorum president I had been told I was responsible for the young men in the teachers quorum. We had one young man who delivered papers on Sunday mornings. His parents were not active. On Sunday mornings I got up and went over to the ward, supervised the preparation of the sacrament, and then walked several blocks to the home of this young man. I rang the doorbell until someone came to the door. I then asked if Gerald was there and whether he was coming to priesthood meeting. Most of the time he was either not back from his paper route or he had gone to bed and his mother said that she would not wake him up. About one out of every four or five times he would be ready and come with me. It is interesting that forty years later I still remember his name and still have an interest in him and wonder how he is doing. I had been trained to go out after those who were not attending and felt they were my responsibility.

Just as truly as the Lord used young men and young women in the past, so he does and will continue to do in our time.

One priest in the Aaronic Priesthood played for his high school football team. In the semifinals of the state tournament, near the end of the game, the quarterback threw a pass to him in the end zone. He dived for the pass and made a great reception. The players on the other team claimed he trapped the ball. The referee ruled that he had caught the ball. That touchdown determined which team won the game and went on to the state finals. After the game, some of the players from the other team came to him and said: "You trapped the ball. Why weren't you honest?" Players from his own team asked him whether he had caught or trapped the ball. He did not answer.

The next morning in priesthood meeting the quorum members asked him whether he had caught or trapped the ball. As before, he did not respond to them. After quorum meeting he went to the bishop's office and asked to see him. He went in, closed the door, and said: "Bishop, you have a right to know whether I caught the ball or trapped it. Bishop, I caught the ball." He felt he needed to share the truth with the bishop, who was the president of the priests quorum.

At Farragut State Park in Idaho last summer, we held mountaintop experiences with the Aaronic Priesthood young men. The General Authorities located in the woods or a couple hundred yards from the road. The young men gathered, an adult leader conducted, and a volunteer opened with prayer. Then the General Authority spoke and answered questions.

About fifteen minutes before I was to speak, four priests came up the trail to hear me. You could hear them two hundred yards away. They sang all the verses of "Redeemer of Israel" (*Hymns,* 1985, no. 6), and then they sang other hymns. They came up to where I was to speak and sat down on the ground right in front of me. They did not try to get to the back where they could fool around or sleep. They really wanted to hear what I had to say. All four of these young men were clean and fine and tall. I believe two of them were twins. After the whole group had arrived, the conducting leader asked if anyone would volunteer to pray. One of the four priests jumped up and said, "I would love to give the prayer." No one prompted him, or begged, or urged. He wanted to pray. I thought, *What a terrific example for the rest of the younger boys who can see this popular young man volunteer and not feel ashamed!*

When I finished speaking, these four young men stayed and asked questions till the next group came. In the next group there was a boy with cerebral palsy in a wheelchair. The other deacon-age Scouts had to carry him in his wheelchair over the rough terrain. They put him right in front of me. Again the conducting officer asked if anyone would volunteer to give the prayer. The palsied boy's great spirit raised his hand. He gave a prayer that was difficult to understand. He slurred each word and had a hard time getting through the prayer. I believe I was on the verge of the interpretation of tongues. I heard every word as clearly as if one of the Brethren were speaking. Here was another great example of someone not ashamed to volunteer to do what he thought the Lord would have him do.

Beloved youth, prepare for your leadership role. A mother prepares her sons and daughters and trains them to fulfill their divine destiny in the future. A man takes that training and becomes a Moses, a Peter, a Joseph, an Apostle, a bishop, a leader in the kingdom. And a woman lives worthily by her mother's example so that she might mother yet another generation of leaders who will startle the world.

The Prophets Speak to Us

The concluding chapter in the book *Les Miserables* is entitled "The Last Drop in the Chalice." It refers to the final purging in the life of Jean Valjean. He is a white-haired saint whose life has been dealt harshly with by law and justice but who was inspired by a Catholic Bishop to be better. This saintly soul, realizing there is one thing left undone to make him a totally honest man, goes through an immense personal struggle and emerges victorious. He does all of this, sacrificing on the altar of love and religion the adoring felicity which Cosette feels toward him who has been all in this life to her. Jean Valjean is convinced that he should unveil before this person, who represents the totality of his reason to live, the dark shadows that cling to his past. With one final resolve he makes all known, aware fully of the expected consequence of alienating the most precious and only soul he has ever loved. The full impact of what I am trying to say can only come as one labors through the 1221-page volume, which I have done five times and again just recently.

I have thought a great deal about President Kimball as I have considered this phrase, "the last drop in the chalice." President Spencer W. Kimball gave more energy, greater service, and had the most profound impact, I think, of anyone in the restored church save the Prophet Joseph only. This was partially due to the numerical size of the Church. It was also due to the shrinking size of the Church through modern means of travel, communication, and increased worldwide acceptance.

President Kimball suffered with problems of boils, throat cancer, heart disease, heart surgery, Bell's palsy, and three subdural hematoma operations. For all that he was publicly known, there are books of deeds which only few know. This saintly man came as near walking in the footsteps of Jesus as any living soul.

Only a few know of the times when he was in the hospital recovering, but took that time to visit others and gave blessings although possibly he had the greater need. I have known and seen brave, faithful men weep as they have talked about President Kimball's visit to their loved ones when all hope seemed lost.

Many unthinking people have gone to his home or to his office, or have cornered him at conference—as if their problems were the only ones in the world that mattered. And this beloved Apostle responded in that very way, as if their problems were the only ones in the world. So many of us who are less than he in the kingdom would have resented the imposition.

I believe he received more letters from members of the Church than any other General Authority. I saw only those that were written to him from members residing in my area, one of thirteen such areas in the world. The letters flowed in regularly and we responded for him.

His office was like a mini-museum of gifts from people who had sent their treasured possessions to share with him. And I think only a small selection of these gifts were displayed in his office.

There were many special trinkets and gifts from those of Lamanite descent. Also, one artist had portrayed the feelings which the minorities especially feel toward President Kimball. There was a beautifully framed rendering of Lamanites and also one of a black family with tears on the cheeks of the father and mother as they gaze toward the Salt Lake Temple. I took a black man and his wife through President Kimball's office and this was the one gift that most impressed them—also to tears.

Consider the giant forward thrust the Church made during the ministry of President Kimball as prophet. President Kimball's great vision reached out before us. He set a work in motion that neither enemy nor foe can frustrate. Compare the majesty of this magnificent soul to the spiritual pygmies who hurl their own faithless frustrations at the Church or try to drag others down to their level of empty faith.

Elder Boyd K. Packer said (speaking of those who persecute the Church), "They leave the Church but they can't leave it alone." They publish theological pornography that is damaging to the spirit. None of it is worth casting an eye on. Do not read the anti-Mormon materials. That is not the way you resolve questions about the truthfulness of the restored gospel. Simply go back and read and ponder and pray about the Book of Mormon and you will know it is true. Those who try to dissuade us from the truth want to tear down what we have but they do not have anything to replace it with. A person who has sexual hang-ups should not read pornographic material as a means of dealing with the problem. Likewise, a person who is weak in the faith should not read "pornographic" theological material. It only destroys and takes away; it never replaces that which was lost.

The names of those who have profited from the sale of anti-Mormon materials will fade and die. Their cause is nonsense. Their hope is desolate and the eternal consequence of attempting to destroy the faith of the Saints will ring everlastingly down through the generations to their own destruction and that of their offspring. The Lord said: "Wherefore, let them bring forth their strong reasons against the Lord. Verily, thus saith the Lord unto you—there is no weapon that is formed against you shall prosper; And if any man lift his voice against you he shall be confounded in mine own due time." (D&C 71:8–10.)

Can we not judge by the Spirit the senselessness of those who splinter the doctrines, rearrange the principles, and ignite the fire of apostasy. We ought to have the wisdom and the vision to see where such nonsensical conduct and teachings lead.

Imagine comparing those shallow, empty minds against the contributions of our prophets. I think there is hardly a congregation that has not sung "We Ever Pray for Thee."

We ever pray for thee with fervent love;
And as the children's prayer is heard above,
Thou shalt be ever blest, and God will give
All that is meet and best while thou shalt live.
                    (*Hymns*, 1985, no. 23.)

We prayed for President Kimball, our noble, beloved prophet of God, as long as he lived. It has been my intention here to share with you some of these thoughts and have you contemplate the final era in the life of President Spencer W. Kimball, which extracted the "last drops of the chalice." And now we pray for this marvelous prophet of God, Ezra Taft Benson, whom we love and honor.

I have tried desperately to consider what the prophets would teach and admonish you if they were in my stead. I have read much of what they have written. I have studied and pondered their talks and I think I have a limited understanding of the style.

I wonder if they wouldn't counsel in this way:

"We have a great spiritual disturbance in our souls. We feel constantly at unrest. It seems that many of our most valiant youth and young adults are falling prey to the deadly tactical warfare of the adversary. Never has there been so much confusion and disruption in our strong Latter-day Saint homes and total abandonment of the principles of truth in others. Hardly a family has not been penetrated to a greater or lesser degree."

I visited a stake in a distant city. I make it a custom to memorize statistics for each stake that I visit, which at least gives me some slight understanding of activity levels. In this stake almost every statistic was down dramatically, including sacrament meeting, priesthood meeting, Relief Society, Primary, Sunday School, youth activity, tithing, and temple activity. I think I had a sense of righteous indignation, maybe even anger, that we had let Satan take over so much real estate.

I questioned the stake leaders and together we prayed and pondered for an answer. It came. This stronghold community of the Church had not especially been aware of the subtleties of Satan's strategy. Many in this farming community had purchased satellite receivers, video shops had opened, and naive parents were either letting R- and X-rated movies into their homes through a satellite channel or the youth and even some parents were renting them. Imagine violating the second most sacred place on the earth, the homes of righteous Latter-day Saints!

I think the prophets would speak boldly against this insidious evil. I think they would counsel parents to monitor what is brought in and out of the home to see that it reflects an LDS standard.

I believe the prophets' hearts would be troubled that Satan is making a mockery of sacred things and that our young people are unsuspectingly being influenced in a more terrible way than they ever would have supposed. We are a peculiar people and that is the strength of this church. We can have our families extended intact into eternity and become like God. I am not ashamed of that. I think it is the most glorious concept ever to be given to man by our God, and I love him for it.

We teach a Word of Wisdom that the modern scientists are discovering is an inspired health law. We have family home evening and family prayer. We pay tithes and offerings and our people prosper. We go to the temple and perform vicarious work for the dead, and we send out our true ambassadors as missionaries to the world. We believe in Christ and we live his commandments, and we do everlastingly many more things as we serve our Lord.

Why then can we not recognize the tactics of the evil one? We should walk in the sun as at noonday.

What Satan has done is perpetrated a great lie upon us. To our youth he has lied: "You can keep your standards but you do not have to be different. You do not need to violate the Word of Wisdom but you do not have to make an issue out of the things that do not really matter." Our very dress and grooming reflects our inward values.

If you will watch and pattern your dress and conduct after the people of real substance, you will not go wrong. Men and women of substance have the inner stability and well-being to follow conservative, inoffensive dress standards. Remember, there is a time and a season for everything under the heavens.

There are different standards of dress for various activities. However, when we are in public, it makes good sense to not groom or dress in a way that will attract undue attention or detract from the surrounding scenery.

I think the prophets might instruct us on the benefits of serving. Robert K. Greenleaf wrote a book entitled *Servant Leadership*. He states:

> The idea of *The Servant as Leader* came out of reading Hermann Hesse's *Journey to the East*. In this story we see a band of men on a mythical journey, probably also Hesse's own journey. The central figure of the story is Leo, who accompanies the party as the *servant* who does their menial chores, but who also sustains them with his spirit and his song. He is a person of extraordinary presence. All goes well until Leo disappears. Then the group falls into disarray and the journey is abandoned. They cannot make it without the servant Leo. The narrator, one of the party, after some years wandering finds Leo and is taken into the Order that had sponsored the journey. There he discovers that Leo, whom he had known first as *servant*, was in fact the titular head of the Order, its guiding spirit, a great and noble leader.
>
> One can muse on what Hesse was trying to say when he wrote this story. We know that most of his fiction was autobiographical, that he led a tortured life, and that *Journey to the East* suggests a turn toward the serenity he achieved in his old age. There has been much speculation by critics on Hesse's life and work, some of it centering on this story which they find the most puzzling. But to me, this story clearly says that *the great leader is seen as servant first*, and that simple fact is the key to his greatness. Leo was actually the leader all of the time, but he was servant first because that was what he was, *deep down inside*. (From *Servant Leadership* by Robert Greenleaf. © 1977 by Robert K. Greenleaf. Used by permission of the Paulist Press.)

Also, Greenleaf states:

> Those who choose to follow this principle will not casually accept the authority of existing institutions. *Rather, they will freely respond only to individuals who are chosen as leaders because they are proven and trusted servants. . . .* My thesis, that more servants should emerge as leaders, or should follow only servant-leaders, is not a popular one. (*Servant Leadership*, p. 10.)

And again:

> The servant-leader *is* servant *first*—as Leo was portrayed. It begins with the natural feelings that one wants to serve, to serve *first*. Then conscious choice brings one to aspire to lead. That person is sharply different from one who is *leader* first. (*Servant Leadership*, p. 13.)

And, finally:

> Not much happens without a dream. And for something great to
> happen, there must be a great dream. Behind every great achieve-
> ment is a dreamer of great dreams. Much more than a dreamer is re-
> quired to bring it to reality; but the dream must be there first.
> (*Servant Leadership*, p. 16.)

> Behold, I say unto you that because I said unto you that I had
> spent my days in your service, I do not desire to boast, for I have
> only been in the service of God.
> And behold, I tell you these things that ye may learn wisdom;
> that ye may learn that when ye are in the service of your fellow
> beings ye are only in the service of your God. (Mosiah 2:16–17.)

The prophets would encourage a sense of humor I believe. I
think you will need it in the days ahead. You may need it in some
of your classes, or on some of your dates, or at work.

I understand that Robbie Bosco (former quarterback for BYU)
is a fighter, that he likes to win. They said one day that he was
carrying a list of all the men he could whip. Leon White (a tough
linebacker on the same team) came up to him and said, "I understand you have a list of all the fellows you can whip." Robbie
said, "That's right." Leon asked "Is my name on that list?"
Robbie responded that it was. Leon White said, "You can't whip
me and I'll prove it." Robbie said, "That's okay. I'll just take your
name off the list."

I heard President Jeffrey Holland of Brigham Young University
refer to the miraculous accomplishments in space that seem
almost commonplace now. It reminded me of a cartoon of two
fleas on a dog. They were leaning against a hair and having a
deep discussion. Off in the distance they saw another dog. One of
them turned to his companion and said, "Do you think there is
life on other dogs?"

Gene Perrett, comedy writer and humorist said, "Humor is
serious business." He is a writer for many of the top comedians.
He shared an experience Bob Hope had:

> Bob Hope was to present an award to a gentleman by the name of
> Charlie Boswell. . . . Charlie Boswell was this country's outstanding
> blind golfer. That's what the award was for. These gentlemen play a
> great game of golf. They have an assistant line the club up, but they

swing themselves, and they hit the ball a ton. They really play a great game.

When he got to the podium, Bob Hope couldn't resist kidding him a little bit. He said, "Outstanding blind golfer, huh. I'd like to play you sometime." Charlie Boswell said, "Mr. Hope, I would love to play you a round of golf." Hope said: "I don't think you understand. I only play for money." Charlie Boswell said: "I like to have a little side bet going, too. It makes things more interesting." And Hope said, "But what kind of a handicap would I have to give you?" Charlie said, "I'll tell you what, Mr. Hope, I'll play you even up." Hope was delighted. He said, "What time?" Charlie Boswell said, "Midnight."

He told a story about Abraham Lincoln:

Abraham Lincoln was once in a debate for public office. His opponent spoke first and Lincoln sat on the platform and listened. His opponent kept pointing to Lincoln and referring to him as a liar, and a cheat, and a two-faced politician. Lincoln never got angry and never showed any emotion. He sat there calmly and listened. When it was his turn to speak, he stepped to the front of the podium and said, "Ladies and gentlemen, if I were two faced, would I be wearing *this one?*"

Then Gene Perrett told about an experience to which some of you may relate:

When my daughter was a sophomore in high school, she'd been wanting to date this one boy. Finally the school sponsored a trip where they rode the train down towards San Diego, had dinner, and took the train back. This gentleman asked her to be his date. I waited up till she got home, and when she came in I asked her, "Honey, how did things go?" She said, "Dad, it's the worst time I ever had in my life." I said: "Why? I thought you were crazy about this guy." She said: "All he did was talk about himself. All the way down, how he plays football, what school he's going to, what he's going to major in. He's the most egotistical person I ever met in my life . . ." I said: "Didn't he see what he was doing? Didn't he realize that all he was doing was talking about himself?" She said: "Just for one brief moment . . . around dessert time. He said to me, 'All I'm doing is talking about myself. How about you. What do you think of me?' " (Gene Perrett, "Humor Is Serious Business: Resist That Urge to Strike Back," *Vital Speeches of the Day* [Southold, New York: City News Publishing Co.], pp. 651–52.)

Then, I think the prophets would tell you of the value of learning to love good and great music. This one great blessing will reward you a thousandfold.

As a bishop, a stake president, or a General Authority, you can sit on the stand and observe the Saints. Music is absolutely an essential element in increasing spirituality. Every Sunday at church when sacred hymns are sung, many in the congregation will quietly weep as they sing. Some have heavy hearts, some have turned their lives back to God and feel his refreshing forgiveness, others have hearts simply filled with the love of God and music has stirred those sensitivities. You will find in life that there is need for a sense of timing and a special awareness that leads you to listen to appropriate music for specific purposes and occasions.

I recently, without any warning or preparation, had a women's chorus sing "We Ever Pray for Thee." The congregation's thoughts were turned to our beloved prophet, Ezra Taft Benson, and tears flowed freely. The choir felt what they sang and deep emotion filled their bosoms. The prophets would want you to make use of good music in your life.

How often the Brethren have reminded us to be pure. Purity of heart is a marvelous quest. "Unto the pure all things [indeed] are pure" (Titus 1:15). The controversy of AIDS, homosexual conduct, and other perversions of life are so constant and common that we almost become sympathetic and understanding to the point of condoning. The gospel of Jesus Christ is for every soul that walks the earth. Its doors of love, purity, charity, and forgiveness are opened wide to all who would enter. But even the great God of heaven cannot save a man in his sins. We sometimes wonder if there are any in the Church who have not been singed by the flames of transgression. Let me say to you: There are hundreds of thousands of our young people who are purer and cleaner than any generation that has walked the earth. To you who are clean, please know you are not alone. God bless you. Continue in that.

President Archie Brugger, president of the San Antonio East Stake in Texas, shared an experience with me that is worthy of your interest. While he served in the military (I believe in Germany), a young officer came to him one day and said, "Colonel Brugger, do you know there are only eight straight arrows in our entire company." A straight arrow is a soldier who does not have an illicit affair with a woman. He said, "I know you are a straight arrow and so am I." A few weeks later this young officer returned again and said, "Colonel Brugger, now there are only four." It was only a matter of a few more weeks and he returned a third time and said, "Colonel Brugger, there are only two, you and me." President Brugger said to this young man: "I intend to remain clean. I am a Mormon and I have a wife back in the United States who is keeping herself clean also while I am away. I trust her and she trusts me and we both honor the teachings of the Church." The young man said: "You are leaving in six weeks to go back to the United States and I will remain here. I don't know how much longer I can hold out." President Brugger said: "My young friend, if I can do it you can do it. The Lord will help you."

In the military there may not be too many straight arrows but I testify to you that in this church there are. I pray you may be one of them. If not, then become one.

I also believe the prophets would want you to love integrity and to honor those who have it. They would want you to use men and women of integrity as models for living. President Nathan Eldon Tanner was known among the Brethren and in the community as Mr. Integrity. But let me say to you that all members of the First Presidency and the Twelve Apostles are the greatest men of integrity I know.

My early family life and business life brought me into association with men who lacked integrity. Sad to say, we also see it in the Church and it breaks our hearts. We see some of our returned missionaries making compromises. Stories come to us about some who have pornographic materials in their apartments, who seemingly went through a two-year mission but the two-year mission did not go through them. Elder Monson was informed of a transgressing missionary in the field. We related the consequences of his conduct—a Church court, dismissal from his mission, family embarrassment, loss of membership, and so on. Elder Monson listened and then said, "The Brethren grieve when they learn of these incidents."

Integrity is honesty to the very center of our souls. It is living what we profess and what we testify. I pray that sometime in the life of every person it may be said, "He or she is a person of integrity."

Prophets of God have often reminded us to practice charity— the pure love of Christ. Charity never faileth. It is the noblest of all virtues. It covereth a multitude of sins. One who has true charity will live every commandment and will love unconditionally. Before charity, all things wash away—pride, impatience, vanity, unkindness, disloyalty, envy, jealousy, uncouthness, unholiness.

Remember, "now abideth faith, hope, charity, these three; but the greatest of these is charity" (1 Corinthians 13:13).

Finally, I think the prophets of the kingdom would say to you, "Become a 'man of Christ,' a disciple of the Master." "Man of Christ" refers to mankind, men and women. Thus we read in Helaman:

> Yea, we see that whosoever will may lay hold upon the word of God, which is quick and powerful, which shall divide asunder all the cunning and the snares and the wiles of the devil, and lead the man of Christ in a strait and narrow course across that everlasting gulf of misery which is prepared to engulf the wicked—
>
> And land their souls, yea, their immortal souls, at the right hand of God in the kingdom of heaven, to sit down with Abraham, and Isaac, and with Jacob, and with all our holy fathers, to go no more out. (Helaman 3:29–30.)

The gospel changes lives.

I know from experience that the values discussed in this book are not only true but are important for successful lives for youth, their parents and leaders. These values can be a guide, a rod of iron to hold on to as one walks the road through life in these challenging times. For this purpose this book was written.

I also know beyond the shadow of a doubt that God lives and that this church is the only authorized agency to function in the name of Jesus Christ. There is no other. I know the Book of

Mormon is true, and I would rather lay down my life this instant than deny that Nephi, King Benjamin, Alma, Ammon, Moroni, Mormon and the brother of Jared were prophets just as were Heber, David, Joseph, Spencer, Harold. Just as Ezra Taft Benson is. The enemies of the Church could line up four abreast from San Francisco to Salt Lake City and come at me to try to convince me that the Church was not true, and when the last one had passed I would still know that this church is Christ's church and that it is true.

Mingling with and listening to the prophets as well as reading their words in holy scriptures have instilled this belief within me. The Holy Ghost has confirmed this witness.

I declare these things in the name of Jesus Christ. Amen.

Index

Friends, 31–37, 83, 148
  of Job, 96–97, 99
Friendship, 14, 31–37, 100
From the Valley of Despair to the Mountain
  Peaks of Hope (pamphlet), 100
Frugality, 88
Frustration, 78
Fujimoto, Shun, 20
Funerals, 75–77
Future, 129–33
Fyans, J. Thomas, 117

– G –

Garfield, Charles, achievements of,
  12–13
  on peak performers, 13
Garvey, Richard C., 28
Genealogical research, 41
General Authorities, 32, 34, 60, 129–30,
  132, 148, 156, 166
Georgia, 87
Gibran, Kahlil, on suffering, 97
God, belief in, 137
  faith of Job in, 92–93
  love of, for his children, 66, 82
Godhead, 49
Go-Getter, The (book), 29
Golf, 164–65
Goliath, 153
Gospel, lives changed by, 16–17
Greatest Thing in the World, The (book),
  26
Greatest Salesman in the World, The
  (book), 29
Greeks, 151–52
Greenleaf, Robert K., Servant Leadership,
  163–64
  on service, 163–64
Grooming. See Dress and grooming

– H –

Habits, 22, 65, 69, 72
Hall, James Norman, Mutiny on the
  Bounty, 29
Handicapped, 7–8, 14, 68, 157
Happiness, 64, 83, 148
Happy Homes and the Hearts That Make
  Them (book), 29, 35, 36, 72–73, 89,
  137
Harding, Warren G., 27
Harris, Dennison, 126–28
Harris, Emer, 126
Harris, Martin, 126

Harrison, Benjamin, on liberty, 16
Hatred, 134
Healings, 155
Health, 95
  mental, 64–65, 69, 134, 148
  physical, 19–21, 23, 65, 69
  through living Word of Wisdom, 71–77
Helaman, 49
Heavenly Father, relationship with, 146
Hesse, Hermann, Journey to the East, 163
"High Flight" (poem), 124
History, 129
Holland, Jeffrey, 164
Holy Ghost, 19, 23, 36
  companionship of, 145, 146
Home, compassion practiced in, 9–11
  financial problems in, 85–86
  See also Families
Home teachers, 69
Homework, 59
Homosexuality, 36, 63, 65–66, 151, 166
Honesty, 19, 56, 60, 68, 85–91, 129–30,
  148
  See also Integrity
Hope, Bob, 164–65
How to Win Friends and Influence People
  (book), 29
Hubbard, Alice, ed., An American Bible,
  58
Hubbard, Elbert Green, on initiative, 58
Hugo, Victor, The Hunchback of Notre
  Dame, 29
  Les Miserables, 29, 39, 80–81, 116, 158
  on quicksand, 80–81
Humility, 4, 56
Humor, 164
"Humor Is Serious Business: Resist That
  Urge to Strike Back" (speech), 165
Hunchback of Notre Dame, The (book), 29
Hurricanes, 102
Hymns, 44, 156, 160–61, 166

– I –

Idaho, 155
Idleness, 67, 69, 151
Idolatry, 153–54
"If" (poem), 135–36
Illness, mental, 64–65, 69, 134, 148
Ingersoll, Robert, on service, 11
Inspiration, 19
Integrity, 4, 57–62, 67, 68, 85–91, 128,
  142, 167–68
  See also Honesty
Intellectual development, 21–23